MAN AND HIS HOPE IN ᴛ⸻
OLD TESTAMENT

STUDIES IN BIBLICAL THEOLOGY

A series of monographs designed to provide clergy and laymen with the best
work in biblical scholarship both in this country and abroad

Advisory Editors:

C. F. D. MOULE, *Lady Margaret's Professor of Divinity
in the University of Cambridge*

PETER ACKROYD, *Samuel Davidson Professor of Old Testament Studies,
University of London*

JAMES BARR, *Professor of Semitic Languages and Literatures,
University of Manchester*

C. F. EVANS, *Professor of New Testament Studies,
King's College, London*

FLOYD V. FILSON, *Formerly Professor of New Testament Literature
and History, McCormick Theological Seminary, Chicago*

G. ERNEST WRIGHT, *Professor of Old Testament History and
Theology at Harvard University*

STUDIES IN BIBLICAL THEOLOGY

Second Series · 20

MAN AND HIS HOPE
IN THE OLD TESTAMENT

WALTHER ZIMMERLI

SCM PRESS LTD
BLOOMSBURY STREET LONDON

Translated from the German
Der Mensch und seine Hoffnung im Alten Testament
(Kleine Vandenhoeck-Reihe 272 S)
Vandenhoeck und Ruprecht, Göttingen 1968

334 00962 6
FIRST PUBLISHED IN ENGLISH 1971
© SCM PRESS LTD 1971
PRINTED IN GREAT BRITAIN BY
W & J MACKAY & CO LTD, CHATHAM

To My Brothers
Nathanael and Ernst
in remembrance of an 80th
and anticipation of a 60th
birthday

CONTENTS

Preface   ix

Abbreviations   xi

  I The Question: The Vocabulary   1

 II Expressions of Hope in Proverbs and the Book of Job   12

III Statements about Hope in the Psalms   26

 IV Man and his Hope according to the Yahwist Writer   42

  V The Bases for the Structure of Hope in the Ancient
Historical Narratives of Israel. The Priestly Account   56

 VI Deuteronomy and the Deuteronomistic History   70

VII The Prophetic Writings of the Eighth Century   86

VIII The Prophecy of the Last Years of Judah and the
Beginning of the Period of the Exile   106

 IX Second Isaiah and the Last of Written Prophecy   122

  X The Hope of Faith according to the Statements of
Apocalyptic   138

 XI Conversation with Ernst Bloch   151

Index of Names   169

Index of References   171

PREFACE

THE eleven lectures presented here, with the exception of the final one, which was never actually delivered, constitute a series of lectures given in the summer of 1967 'for the members of all faculties'. The impetus for this series arose from study of Ernst Bloch's use of the Old Testament. The conversation with Ernst Bloch in the last chapter (even within the very limited framework dictated by the general theme) should not be understood as a mere frill, but as – even with the real difference of viewpoint – a grateful reference to this man who, with his passionate utterances about the 'principle of hope', has compelled the student of the Old Testament to give a fresh account of the basis of statements about hope in the Bible. Because the lectures were directed towards a fairly wide circle of listeners from all faculties, I have avoided discussions of a technical nature in the narrowest sense. The notes will give further reference material to the reader who desires more information about the Old Testament texts discussed. The reproduction of the Old Testament text, for the basis of which I refer the reader to the appropriate literature and the apparatus of the third edition of the *Biblia Hebraica* of Rudolf Kittel, often depends, as the observant reader will detect, upon the translation of the Zürich Bible, for which we may largely thank the quiet work of my teacher and predecessor in the chair of Old Testament at Zürich, Jakob Hausheer.* Otherwise wherever the original text of the Old Testament uses the word Yahweh as the name for God, this has been retained in the translation. The transcription of the proper names also follows the Zürich Bible. For assistance with corrections I wish to thank my assistant, Dr Christian Jeremias.

WALTHER ZIMMERLI

* This translation uses the Revised Standard Version of the Bible, except where Dr Zimmerli's argument requires an approximate English rendering of his own German translation of the biblical text, and except for the use of 'Yahweh' in the places indicated above.

ABBREVIATIONS

ATANT	Abhandlungen zur Theologie des Alten und Neuen Testaments, Zürich
ATD	Das Alte Testament Deutsch, Göttingen
BKAT	Biblischer Kommentar. Altes Testament, Neukirchen
BWANT	Beiträge zur Wissenschaft vom Alten und Neuen Testament, Stuttgart
BZAW	Beiheft zur *Zeitschrift für die alttestamentliche Wissenschaft*, Berlin
ET	English translation
EvTh	*Evangelische Theologie*, Munich
FRLANT	Forschungen zur Religion und Literatur des Alten und Neuen Testaments, Göttingen
HAT	Handbuch zum Alten Testament, Tübingen
KAT	Kommentar zum Alten Testament, Gütersloh
KlSchr	A. Alt, *Kleine Schriften zur Geschichte des Volkes Israel*, Munich, Vols. I–II, 1953, Vol. III, 1959
OTL	Old Testament Library, London and Philadelphia
RB	*Revue Biblique*, Paris
SBT	Studies in Biblical Theology, London and Naperville
SVT	Supplements to *Vetus Testamentum*, Leiden
TDNT	*Theological Dictionary of the New Testament*, Grand Rapids, Michigan
ThB	Theologische Bücherei, Munich
TLZ	*Theologische Literaturzeitung*, Leipzig
TWNT	*Theologisches Wörterbuch zum Neuen Testament*, Stuttgart
TZ	*Theologische Zeitschrift*, Basel
WMANT	Wissenschaftliche Monographien zum Alten und Neuen Testament, Neukirchen
ZAW	*Zeitschrift für die alttestamentliche Wissenschaft*, Berlin
ZST	*Zeitschrift für systematische Theologie*, Gütersloh and Berlin
ZTK	*Zeitschrift für Theologie und Kirche*, Tübingen

I

THE QUESTION: THE VOCABULARY

In our time man has made dramatic strides forward in the conquest of his environment. The prospects that open before us of a technical mastery of the material world, the life processes, and even space are enough to make one's head spin.

But who can say that man has mastered himself and the mystery of his own being as he has his environment? In the midst of all his technical prowess, he is more than ever engaged in the search for himself. In the last century he could rest secure in a world held together by the great designs of idealist philosophy, but in our day he has been frightened out of this refuge. The terrible awakening of the post-war years created a new hearing for the existentialist understanding of man with its experience of anxiety and vulnerability. What is there about the nature of man? Is it not peculiarly marked by an existence toward death, a transiency in which man can only be said really to live in the decision of the moment? Is there any real continuity to historical life beyond the moment of decision?

In the light of all this, the question about the possibility of a future for mankind must be asked in a new and more fundamental way. Does man, so deeply threatened in his own existence, confronted by new and all-embracing threats, hitherto unknown, arising as they do out of all the possibilities presented him by science and technology, seriously possess the possibility of a future and a hope? In this situation Ernst Bloch's great philosophical masterpiece, *Das Prinzip Hoffnung*,[1] dealing as it does not only with mankind but also with his environment, including the surrounding natural world, its history and predisposition towards a future and towards hope, fell into well-prepared soil. This book, so richly illustrated from the whole intellectual history of mankind and not least with special reference to the Old Testament, quickly stirred up a lively discussion, particularly in the theological arena.[2]

The key-word 'hope' is admittedly no discovery of modern man as he looks about him for help in the midst of a threatened existence. It is amply offered by the Christian faith from New Testament times onwards. Here the words *elpis*, 'hope', and *elpizein*, 'to hope', play a not insignificant role. Further, in his investigation of these words Bultmann[3] has clarified their use in Greek literature. The root word, whose stem *welp-* is associated with the Latin *velle*, 'to want', and *voluptas*, 'the [wished for] pleasure', developed in the Greek the near universal meaning of 'expectation' in relation to the future. The more precise meaning was made clear by the use of an adjective, indicating either a good expectation (*elpis agathē, glykeia, hilarā, chrēstē*) or a bad expectation (*elpis kakē*).[4] Man could be admonished not to give in to the misleading visions created by his expectations. 'Only a god does not err in his expectations, and men's *elpides* are uncertain,' concludes Bultmann of the Greek world.[5] Against this background the mythical tale of Pandora's box, with which Hesiod begins his *Works and Days*, can be understood in its original meaning. *Elpis* always remains for man a treacherous expectancy. 'Hope and danger are similar so far as man is concerned. Both are evil demons,' says Theognis (637f.)[6]. As a stimulation for human efficiency (*techne*) hope has, of course, its great value. But hope is blind – so says the chained Prometheus of Aeschylus with complete candour. His exchange with the chorus, leading to this conclusion, runs thus:

Pr.   From thoughts of coming death I saved mankind.
Ch.   What medicine for that sickness couldst thou find?
Pr.   Blind hopes I planted in their hearts to dwell.[7]

In contrast the New Testament use of the words *elpis* and *elpizein* reveals a different emphasis. First, it is apparent that quite apart from any predicate, hope always points to a positive expectation on man's part, to something which, as the basic root of the word itself suggests, man really wants for himself.

To come down to details, we find here on the one hand an unreflective and everyday use of the word. For example, I Cor. 9.10, in dealing with the Old Testament commandment against muzzling the ox that is threshing,[8] and the notion that man is worth his wage, says that whoever ploughs, ploughs in hope, and whoever threshes, threshes in hope, that he may share in the crop. Here hope refers to the simple expectation of the worker that he will receive the reward of his labours.

On the other hand there emerges in the New Testament a characteristically theological way of speaking about hope. The noun does not occur in the Gospels and Revelation but is especially common in writings of Paul or those influenced by him. Hope is used here in a highly specialized sense and in connection with faith in God. Remembering the pre-Christian situation of the Ephesians, the Letter to the Ephesians can say that they were without hope and without God (*atheoi*); cf. also I Thess. 4.13. Thus we are confronted with utterances about hope which are always very precise in meaning and which stand in close relationship to the salvation God has effected in Christ. In sharp contrast to what Prometheus said about it, hope is here understood as certain and dependable – that which never comes to nothing or disappoints, even as it is spoken of as the final link in the chain of Rom. 5.3–5:

We know that suffering produces endurance, and endurance produces character, and character produces hope. And hope does not disappoint us because God's love has been poured into our hearts through the Holy Spirit which has been given to us.

Here hope has nothing to do with that vague human expectation that springs from Pandora's box as a doubtful blessing. It is rather the certain strength of faith which lives from the love of God as it is poured into human hearts by the Spirit of God. In this light it becomes understandable that in Paul (I Cor. 13.13) hope appears in that great triad of 'faith, hope, and love', all of which remain even when the patchwork of a passing world is gone. If, therefore, hope is very near to faith, and is, to a degree, an aspect of faith, as is basically the case in the great statements about hope in Rom. 8, so conversely Heb. 11 can depict faith by reference to hope: 'Now faith is the assurance of things hoped for, the conviction of things not seen.' And then there is the well-known word of I Peter 3.15 which admonishes, 'Always be prepared to make a defence to any one who calls you to account for the hope that is in you.' Here also the word hope is clearly interchangeable with the word faith.

Thus statements about hope occupy a central position in the New Testament.

But now let us leave these New Testament statements, and turn our attention to the first part of the Bible, the Old Testament.[9]

First we must ask what this earlier part of the Bible, ignorant as it is of the name of Jesus Christ upon whom in the New Testament all hope is based, has to say about man and his hope.

It will be well if first we briefly consider and make clear the double usage of the word 'hope' as this is apparent even in any brief introductory explanations of the word. The verb 'to hope' and the noun 'hope' derived from it point first of all to a human act similar to love and faith. It is an attitude of expectancy which, as the extra-biblical understanding of *elpizein* demonstrates, can be dealt with in a purely formal manner quite apart from its object, receiving in many cases further content for good or ill by the object toward which it is directed. On the other hand the noun hope can take on such strong content from the direction in which a man hopes, that his attitude passes over into that which is the object of hope. For example, when a shipwrecked sailor, driven by the sea, catches sight of a life-boat and knows that 'this boat is my hope', then all reference to the subjective state of mind of the sailor struggling in the sea is lost. The hope of the man in the water is here so fixed on the approaching instrument of salvation that everything else retreats and he identifies that which exists outside himself as his hope, that is, as the peculiar object and content of his hope. Thus statements about hope move linguistically back and forth between these two possible understandings and can in individual cases be confined to one or the other: hope as an attitude within man and hope as something which approaches man, which is projected toward this attitude in man to the point that all thought of his own mental processes is forgotten. Thus does our language discourse about hope.

If, after these preliminary considerations, we look to the statements of the Old Testament, we encounter at the very outset a situation of unexpected difficulty. In Greek there is no question that the noun *elpis* and the verb *elpizein* are the objects of our investigation. These are the particular words which express what we mean by 'hope' and 'to hope'.

But if we approach the Hebrew of the Old Testament expecting to find an equally simple state of affairs, we discover instead a situation which is far more ambiguous. This can immediately be seen from a glance at the two Hebrew-German Lexicons most in use at the present.

Taking up first that of Ludwig Koehler,[10] we discover in the final summary that for the verb 'to hope' only a single Hebrew equivalent is identified,[11] the verb *šbr* in the intensive stem. This verb is twice verified as having the meaning 'to inspect, examine' in the basic stem form. According to Neh. 2.13, 15, Nehemiah, sent from the Persian court to Jerusalem, in a secret night ride 'inspects' the condition of the ruins of the city walls. In the intensive stem the verb has the accent of waiting, hopeful watching. There are altogether six examples of this usage, of which the one in Ruth 1.13 should be translated simply as 'waiting'. Here Naomi says to both daughters-in-law, who wish to go with her after the death of her two sons and whom she advises to return to their own people: 'Even if I should have a husband this night and should bear sons, would you therefore wait till they were grown?' In the remaining five instances the emphasis on 'hopeful watching' is more clearly evident, as in the expression that appears in Ps. 145.15: 'The eyes of all look to thee and thou givest them their food in due season' (also with slight variations in wording in Ps. 104.27). Here 'look' undoubtedly means 'watch hopefully'. Cf. also Ps. 119.166, Isa. 38.18, and Esth. 9.1.

According to Koehler the instances of the noun 'hope' are somewhat more numerous. Beside the two examples of the noun *šēber* from the verb *šbr* already mentioned (Pss. 119.116; 146.5), and the three examples of the noun *mabbāt*, which translated literally means 'an (expectant, hopeful) watching', or 'that toward which one looks (expectantly, hopefully), Koehler points out three other substantives: two of them (*miqweh* and *tiqwāh*) are from one verb *qwh*, the third, *tohelet* is derived from the verb *yhl*. Koehler translates both verbs by 'wait'. Whereas there are five examples of the noun *miqweh* with the meaning 'hope' and six such examples of *tohelet*, the substantive *tiqwāh* occurs more frequently. A biblical Aramaic equivalent for the noun 'hope' does not exist.

A consideration of the proposed equivalents for hope in Koehler's Lexicon leaves us with two questions. First there is the somewhat surprising question: is it possible that the Old Testament really speaks so sparingly as far as verbal formulation goes about man's hope? Closer examination further reveals that the single verb identified by Koehler, the verb *šbr*, apparently belongs to later language and played an important role in Aramaic and late Hebrew. Is it possible that the earlier periods knew nothing about 'hoping'? And in this connection there comes the second question:

is it possible that the two verbs, which stand behind the nouns *miqweh* and *tiqwāh* on the one hand and the noun *toḥelet* on the other, have no relationship to the activity of hope?

This leads us to the statements of the second Hebrew-German lexicon, which was first produced by Wilhelm Gesenius in Halle at the beginning of the last century, of which the latest edition, revised by Buhl, appeared in 1915.[12] Here we discover in the German-Hebrew index at the end of the volume four equivalents for the German word 'to hope'. Besides *śbr*, also mentioned by Koehler, there are also two verbs anticipated by our second question put to the Koehler lexicon. The first is *qwh* whose basic stem Gesenius-Buhl understand as 'to wait, to hope', whereas they note only the meaning 'to wait' for the intensive stem. However, in its repeated association with Yahweh it too carries unmistakably with it the accent of hope. The second is *yḥl*; for the rendering of this verb the meaning 'to wait' is also proposed for both intensive and causative stems. Only in Ps. 119.49 ought the intensive stem to be rendered as 'to cause to hope'. But one could make the same observation about this verb as about the verb *qwh*. As a fourth instance there is mention of the verb *ṣph*, which means first 'to watch, to observe intently, to look out for', but whose intensive stem is best rendered in Micah 7.7, according to the lexicographers, with 'to hope'. When we read: 'But as for me, I will look (*ṣph*) to Yahweh, I will wait (*yḥl*) for the God of my salvation', hopeful watching is clearly what is expressed.

If Gesenius-Buhl draw the circle around the verbs which give expression to hope wider than Koehler, the same applies to the noun 'hope'. To the five equivalents proposed by Koehler, Gesenius-Buhl add five more which are admittedly not all equally specific in meaning. When for instance the word *šaḥar*, 'dawn', is translated as 'hope' in Isa. 8.20, we are obviously dealing with a metaphorical and derivative use of the word. The word *morāš* in Job 17.11 means 'wish' according to its etymological derivation. But here the context demands the translation 'hope'. Hope includes not only a waiting but also a wishing. And the next word introduced by Gesenius-Buhl also has its own peculiar meaning independent of the meaning of hope. *'aḥᵃrit* means originally 'the back side', then 'the exit, the end of an epoch, the end result, the future'. In connection with the happy end of a matter toward which man strives, in three instances (Jer. 29.11; Prov. 23.18;

24.14) it very clearly takes on the unambiguous meaning of 'hope' and is connected with or set in parallel with *tiqwāh*. Hope is reaching out toward a future in which a good ending is anticipated. Both of the other proposed equivalents lead in a completely different direction: *biṭṭāḥon* means according to its obvious derivation 'trust' and similarly *kislāh*, 'confidence'. In Job 4.6 where the oldest of the friends of Job admonishes him: 'Is not your fear of God your confidence (*kislāh*), and the integrity of your ways your hope?' (*tiqwāh*), the wording of the parallelism clearly makes the emphasis on hope dominant. Here it is a matter of confident waiting for that which fear of God gives, the hope that is present in the fear of God. The passage in Eccles. 9.4, where *biṭṭāḥon*, 'trust', can only be translated with the word 'hope' to do full justice to its meaning, will concern us more directly in a later connection. It is a matter of the same line of thought when Gesenius-Buhl propose that the verb *šlh*, which has as a primary meaning 'to be quiet, secure', should in its causative use in II Kings 4.28 be translated as 'to delude someone about something so as to awaken hope'. Hope can make a man confident and full of trust and yet also wrongly make him gullible.

Surveying the general results of this investigation into both lexicographers, we are confronted even at this cursory first glance with two very clear conclusions.

First, we can see quite clearly even from this superficial lexicographic approach to our subject that the Old Testament beyond any doubt knows something about hope and in its various parts speaks of hope.

But we see with equal clarity that in contrast to the New, the Old Testament does not achieve a clearly fixed terminology for 'to hope' and 'hope', as in the analogy of the New Testament *elpis* and *elpizein* where a root word takes to itself a decisive content. There is in the Old Testament no clear and exclusively fixed concept for 'to hope' or 'hope'. The nearest thing to this would be the two substantives *tiqwāh* and *toḥelet*. But even these do not reach the rank of firmly fixed theological concepts, but receive their particular emphasis from the verb stems that stand behind them. Thus in the Old Testament the various aspects of the meaning of 'hope', as they are brought to expression by various words, exist side by side. Right in the foreground is the aspect of waiting and tarrying (derivatives of the roots *qwh, yḥl, śbr*, to which basically the root *ḥkh*, 'to wait', should also be added). Viewed as a human attitude, hope is a waiting, an existence toward that which is to come. With the word *qwh* one might perhaps add the note of internal strain. The substantive *tiqwāh*, meaning 'cord' or 'rope', is constructed from the same root, and there is also the shorter *qaw* with the identical meaning.[13] This tense expectant watchfulness is also seen in *ṣph*. The scout, who stands on the city wall and must look sharply for any approaching danger, is called *ṣopeh*. In contrast *yḥl*, 'to wait', does not appear to project any of this kind of tension. It rather simply presupposes the condition of 'not yet' in which a man waits for what is coming and is oriented toward the event of its coming. Thus Noah, for example, when he sent out a bird after the flood, waited seven days, and then investigated the changing situation by trying something else. *ḥkh* also appears to have this emphasis. In contrast to these, *'aḥªrît*, 'the end', brings to full expression the note of the 'future moment'. The object toward which hope reaches lies at the end of a time span characterized by the tension of waiting and involves something of result and goal. That this goal is desirable comes to expression with the word *morāš*, 'wish'. By contrast another stress is brought forward with the words *biṭṭāḥon*, 'trust', and *kislāh*, 'confidence'. Here there is the suggestion that man, when he hopes, gives himself over to what is coming, places his trust in it and holds out for it, wins for himself certitude, yes, even certainty, as can be seen in the use of *šlh* in this connection.

Now it is also advisable to approach the question of terminology from another side. We have moved from New Testament discourse about hope, with its precise terminology of *elpis* and *elpizein*, to the question of the situation in the Old Testament. The Greek New Testament is, however, terminologically very close to the Septuagint, the Greek version of the Hebrew and Aramaic Old Testament. So it becomes advisable, at the close of these preliminary clarifications of the linguistic questions, to take a look also at the Greek Old Testament in which the *elpis-elpizein* terminology is found. In all the canonical books (though not in the Apocrypha which is transmitted only in Greek) there is the possibility of comparing the basic Hebrew text with the Greek translation and asking the question: which Hebrew equivalents does the Greek translator believe he must translate by *elpis* and *elpizein*? As well as listening to the modern lexicographers, we ought not to pass over these earliest attempts to determine equivalents with corresponding meaning. But here there comes a surprise. The Septuagint does not take the same direction as that taken by contemporary lexicographers. The differences in treatment are most apparent in the case of the verbal forms used for the word 'hope'. Of the hundred instances where the Hebrew equivalent for *elpizein* can be determined, no less than forty-seven, that is, almost half, are given over to the rendering of the Hebrew word *bṭḥ* (or in one instance the adverb *beṭaḥ*), a word for which the modern lexicographers have not in one single instance proposed the translation 'hope'. In the one case in which the noun *biṭṭāḥon* is translated by 'hope', there is in the text a connection between the root *bṭḥ*, which we are accustomed to translate by 'trust', and the word 'hope'. In twenty further instances *elpizein* in the Septuagint appears as the rendering of *ḥsh* in the Hebrew text – another parallelism which we do not encounter in modern lexicographers. They translate *ḥsh* as 'to protect oneself, seek refuge'. Of the four verbs that Gesenius-Buhl consider to be possible equivalents for 'to hope', *śbr* is rendered as *elpizein* in the Septuagint in two instances, *qwh* also in only two, *ṣph* never, and *yḥl* somewhat more often, that is, in thirteen cases, six of which actually give *epelpizein*.

When we come to the rendering of the nouns for 'hope', the Septuagint and modern lexicographers stand closer together. Thus in the books of Job and Proverbs *elpis* is consistently used to translate *tiqwāh*, and outside these books other Greek words appear. Here too in twenty-seven cases *elpis* is used to translate a derivative of the root *bṭḥ*, 'trust'.

At this point I can leave further consideration of details. The general picture is, in any case, completely clear in its central thrust. The translators of the Septuagint have found statements of hope primarily where the thought is of trust and refuge in God. They therefore agree in describing as decisive and most important that aspect of hope which involves the moment of personal surrender. 'Hope' is not in the first place a situation of tension toward the future, a wish or the indication of a goal that one awaits with tension – it is above all, and the Septuagint emphasizes this very strongly, a situation of surrender and trust, which naturally cannot be realized in a vacuum but which requires one who stands over against us and calls us to trust.

But enough of these preliminary linguistic remarks. It is now our task to listen to the substance of the statements of the Old Testament and from them to recognize not only the description but also the foundation of Old Testament discourse about hope. Old Testament faith reckons with the future. It is more than just a coincidence that it is precisely the people of the Old Testament, who far more than any other experienced death and the threat of death again and again, who never give up hope in the future. The country which has arisen in our time under the name 'Israel', labels its national anthem with the word *tiqwāh*, 'hope'. How do the individual Old Testament writings speak of hope? That is the question that will concern us in the following chapters.

NOTES

¹ Ernst Bloch, *Das Prinzip Hoffnung* (Gesamtausgabe Band 5, Frankfurt am Main 1959), written in the USA between 1938 and 1947, revised 1953 and 1959.
² Cf. e.g. J. Moltmann, *Theology of Hope* (ET of 5th ed., London 1967), and further *Diskussion über die 'Theologie der Hoffnung' von Jürgen Moltmann*, ed. W. D. Marsch (Munich 1967); also G. Sauter, *Zukunft und Verheissung. Das Problem der Zukunft in der gegenwärtigen theologischen und philosophischen Diskussion* (Zürich-Stuttgart 1965); see esp. notes on pp. 279–81, which list, in addition to Bloch's own work on the question, the most important comments on Bloch up to 1963.
³ *TDNT* II, pp. 517ff.
⁴ *Ibid*, p. 518 n. 5.
⁵ *Ibid.*, pp. 519f.
⁶ Cited in *TDNT* II, p. 519 n. 10.
⁷ Aeschylus, *Prometheus Bound*, lines 248–50, trans. Gilbert Murray (London 1931).
⁸ Deut. 25.4.
⁹ The question as it relates to the Old Testament has undergone surprisingly little investigation. Cf. e.g. C. Westermann, 'Das Hoffen im Alten Testament. Eine Begriffsuntersuchung', *Theologia Viatorum* IV (Jahrbuch der Kirchlichen Hochschule Berlin, 1953), pp. 19–70, reprinted in *Forschung am Alten Testament* (ThB 24, 1964), pp. 219–65; T.C. Vriezen, 'Die Hoffnung im Alten Testament', *TLZ* 78 (1953), cols. 577–87; J. van der Ploeg, 'L'espérance dans l'Ancien Testament', *RB* 61 (1954), pp. 481–507. In the Index to L. Koehler, *Old Testament Theology* (ET of 3rd ed., London 1957), the word is completely absent. In W. Eichrodt, *Theology of the Old Testament* I (ET of 6th ed., OTL 1961), there are only ten references for 'Messianic Hope' (an improvement on the three in the German original), and in Vol. II (ET of 5th ed. of Parts 2/3, OTL 1967) the word is completely absent. The same is true of G. von Rad, *Old Testament Theology* I (ET of 2nd ed., Edinburgh 1962), while in the Index to Vol. II (ET 1965) there are two references (to Jeremiah and Second Isaiah). A study preliminary to the material presented here can be found in my

contribution to *Studia Biblica et Semitica Theodoro Christiano Vriezen* . . . *dedicata* (Wageningen 1966), pp. 389–403. Cf. also H. D. Preuss, *Jahweglaube und Zukunftserwartung* (BWANT 5.7, 1968).

[10] L. Koehler-W. Baumgartner, *Lexicon in Veteris Testamenti libros* (Leiden 1953). [So also F. Brown, S. R. Driver and C. A. Briggs, *A Hebrew and English Lexicon of the Old Testament* (Oxford 1907, reprinted with corrections 1953 and 1957). Translator]

[11] In the Aramaic section of Koehler-Baumgartner there is no equivalent.

[12] Wilhelm Gesenius, *Hebräisches und aramäisches Handwörterbuch über das Alte Testament,* 17th ed. revised by F. Buhl (Leipzig 1915, reprinted 1954).

[13] P. de Boer, on the other hand, works out another classification in his 'Étude sur la racine qwh', *Oudtestamentische Studiën* X (1954), pp. 225–46.

II

EXPRESSIONS OF HOPE IN PROVERBS AND
THE BOOK OF JOB

A PERUSAL of the vocabulary of the Old Testament has revealed
that in contrast to the New Testament it knows no exclusive,
linguistically fixed terminology for hope and hoping. Granted,
some words in their substantive form, derived from the verbs for
waiting and tarrying, are central to the Old Testament. But around
these there extend other expressions which open up entirely different aspects of hope.

It is advisable to tackle first the individual statements of the Old
Testament about hope under the guidance of the vocabulary we
have uncovered in order later to cut ourselves loose from this
vocabulary and ask entirely on the basis of content what the Old
Testament says about the hopeful expectation which its faith sees
as opening up the future. Now a glance at the concordance reveals
that both of the most important nouns, *tiqwāh* and *toḥelet*, are
especially prominent in the books of Proverbs and Job. No less
than twenty-one out of a total of thirty-one examples of *tiqwāh*
bearing the meaning of 'hope', and four of the six examples of
toḥelet, are to be found in these books.

This is more than a pure accident of statistics. In Proverbs, and
in a broader sense also in the book of Job, we are dealing with
documents classified as wisdom literature.[1] 'Wisdom' has to do
with an open look at the world and above all at human life and its
particular impulses. Here it makes its observations, seeks here to
recognize the laws governing the course of the world and human
life, so that it may formulate its directions for life on the basis of
these observations. We know now more fully than we did a few
decades ago that this Old Testament wisdom does not simply pass
on the natural common sense of man, but has passed through a
conscious artistic development and includes definite cultural con-

tent. We know too that it stands in international relationship to equivalents in Egypt as well as in Babylonia, and before that in ancient Sumer. Such a venture on the part of man into investigation of the world and the possibility of mastering life within it, will not be able to overlook the phenomenon of hope. Hope, knowledge about the openness of the future, belongs inseparably to the possibility of a full life for man. It plays no small role in individual sectors of human life.

Thus we can observe in fact in Proverbs[2] how the wise man confronts the human phenomenon of hope with his models of and contemplation of the world. He makes his psychological observations completely from the outside. Prov. 13.12 observes: 'Hope (*tohelet*, waiting) deferred makes the heart sick, but a desire (*ta'awāh*) is a tree of life [that is something that makes life fresh and new].' Prolonged, futile hoping and waiting depresses a man's frame of mind and his health. This is what is very sensibly asserted here.

Other places speak of the possibility of hope in a definite area of life – for instance, Prov. 19.18 in the sphere of education:

> Discipline your son while there is hope:
> do not set your heart on his destruction.

Behind this statement stands the conviction that an ill-advised son is in danger for his life, because he is headed in a direction which threatens with death if he does not turn from it. But at the same time a thorough-going optimism about education is affirmed here, insisting that there is hope as long as the young man is malleable and can be brought to the correct road by means of rigid discipline, as exemplified by Egyptian educational methods.[3] On the basis of this hope the father should deal with his son and so not become responsible for his destruction.

Other rules embracing the whole of life and its hope dominate even more vigorously the realm of wisdom literature. In Prov. 10.28 we read:

> The hope (*tohelet*) of the righteous ends in gladness,
> but the expectation (*tiqwāh*) of the wicked comes to naught.

Here the true and false hopes of life are dealt with and the conclusion reached that only the righteous man has authentic hope that will be fulfilled to his joy, whereas the godless man is frustrated in his life's expectations and has no future. In addition there is behind these sentences the optimistic certainty that hope does have its rights in human life, its proper expectations. But whether human hope really has this prospect in life, depends upon a man's own decisions about life – whether he holds to the pattern of righteousness or whether he high-handedly does unjustly and (this stands behind it) does not want to know anything of God. We might also wonder whether this thought is not also expressed in Prov. 11.23 :

> The desire (*ta'ᵃwāh*) of the righteous ends only in good;
>   the expectation (*tiqwāh*) of the wicked in wrath.

According to this word too, human righteousness or unrighteousness determines whether the hope of a given life has authenticity. This point of view can be transformed in other places into the direct admonition:

> Let not your heart envy sinners [the thought here is of that envy
>   that is jealous of the good fortune of sinners],
>   but continue in the fear of the Lord all the day.
> Surely [when you continue to do so] there is a future
>   (*'aḥᵃrīt*),
>   and your hope (*tiqwāh*) will not be cut off.
>   (Prov. 23.17f.)

In Prov. 24.19f. the reason given for identical admonition is changed to 'for the evil man has no future [hope, *'aḥᵃrīt*]; the lamp of the wicked will be put out.' The very similar admonition of Ps. 37, one of the Wisdom Psalms, draws a comparison in v. 1 between the destruction of wrongdoers and the withering grass. The reason given in Prov. 23.18 is almost word for word the same as in the otherwise very different construction of Prov. 24.13f., where we find, in one of the common substitutions of Proverbs, wisdom put in place of the fear of God. This substitution is introduced with a word picture:

> My son, eat honey, for it is good,
>   and the drippings of the honeycomb are sweet to your taste.
> Know that wisdom is such to your soul [to you];
>   if you find it, there will be a future (*'aḥᵃrīt*),
>   and your hope (*tiqwāh*) will not be cut off.

Behind all these expressions lies a faith in a fixed order in the world, in which the righteousness and wisdom of man, always viewed realistically in connection with his earthly life, give him a future and a hope. On the other hand, when Prov. 26.12 says,

Do you see a man who is a wise in his own eyes?
There is more hope (*tiqwāh*) for a fool than for him,

and similarly Prov. 29.20 says,

Do you see a man who is hasty in his words?
There is more hope (*tiqwāh*) for a fool than for him,

this does not mean that the possibility of hope for a fool is reintroduced and he is now promised a future. Rather this is said completely within the over-all viewpoint that a fool has no hope. This is the order that rules in the world.

We are here speaking within the framework of the more recent discussions of wisdom literature,[4] which deal with the thought of Egyptian wisdom literature, where at this point the concept of *maat* appears, that is, of the truth or order represented by a divinity. Apparently this world of *maat*, of order, is also presupposed by the biblical wisdom literature. Naturally here in the Old Testament context the deity that guarantees this world-order is no other than Yahweh himself. Thus Prov. 20.22 says,

Do not say, 'I will repay evil';
wait for the Yahweh, and he will help you.

The guarantee of order, which sets man free from the necessity of having to seek his own revenge, rests with Yahweh alone. Upon him the devout man must wait. But such waiting is impossible without trust. And here we are confronted with the view of hope which stands so strongly in the foreground in the translation of the Septuagint. For example, in Prov. 14.26, which reads, 'In the fear of Yahweh one has strong confidence (that is, fear of Yahweh gives a strong faith), and his children will have a refuge,' the Septuagint translates the Hebrew *mibṭaḥ*, 'trust', with *elpis*, 'In the fear of the Lord one has a strong hope.' The word spoken by personified wisdom in Prov. 1.33, 'But he who listens to me will dwell secure [literally: in faith]' reads in the Greek text: 'But he who listens to me will dwell in hope (*ep' elpidi*).' And in the same way in Prov. 22.19 the Greek speaks of hope in the Lord, where the Hebrew speaks of trust in Yahweh.

Turning now from Proverbs to the book of Job,[5] we come up

against a surprising and highly critical argument against the phenomenon of hope and the possibility of speaking of a hope for man.
First a brief word about the setting of the book of Job. In this
piece of writing, originating in the post-exilic period, there is
portrayed, within a narrative framework beginning with chs. 1–2
and ending in ch. 42, a devout man who has lived in fear of God.
This narrative framework recounts conversations that take place
between God and Satan, who is here considered one of the ser-
vants of God who acts primarily to disclose the hidden guilt of
men. In order to bring to light the true quality of Job's piety, the
devout Job, at the instigation of Satan, is assaulted by all kinds of
misfortune. He loses all that he has, even his health, so that finally
he sits struck down by disaster on a heap of ashes and scratches his
sores with a potsherd. Here, after rejecting the tempting words of
his wife, he receives a visit from three friends who first sit silent
with him for seven days and share his misery. Then Job opens his
mouth, curses the day he was born, and cries out in his misery.
This sets the friends talking. So finally we come to the conversation between Job and his friends, a later addition to the original
story. Naturally these friends do not know the secret of the
heavenly wager between God and Satan. The words of a fourth
friend, Eliphaz, in chs. 32–37 are an addition of an even later
period. These speeches consider the possibility of hope for Job
and for mankind generally.

We do well to listen first to the words of the friends. It is immediately clear that the first one, Eliphaz the Temanite, obviously
the calmest and most thoughtful of the three friends, intends to try
and comfort the stricken Job. He reminds Job of how he himself
would once comfort the afflicted:

> But now it has come to you, and you are impatient;
>   it touches you, and you are dismayed.
> Is not your fear of God your confidence,
>   and the integrity of your ways your hope (*tiqwāh*)?
> Think now, who that was innocent ever perished?
>   Or where were the upright cut off?
> As I have seen, those who plough iniquity
>   and sow trouble reap the same.
> By the breath of God they perish,
>   and by the blast of his anger they are consumed.
>   (Job 4.5–9)

And somewhat later there follows the advice:

> As for me, I would seek God,
>   and to God would I commit my cause:
> who does great things and unsearchable,
>   marvellous things without number:
> he gives rain upon the earth
>   and sends waters upon the fields;
> he sets on high those who are lowly
>   and those who mourn are lifted to safety.
> He frustrates the devices of the crafty,
>   so that their hands achieve no success.
> He takes the wise in their own craftiness . . .
> But he saves the fatherless from their mouth,
>   the needy from the hand of the mighty.
> So the poor have hope,
>   and injustice shuts her mouth. (Job 5.8–16)

It is clear that Eliphaz wants to comfort Job with these words even as he himself has earlier comforted others. In his words of consolation he recommends that Job put his troubles in God's hands, the God who does not leave the devout and the weak without help. The devout man may depend upon this. It is not difficult to recognize behind this consolation the attitude of the wisdom that is also found in Proverbs. It is expressed by Eliphaz in a markedly elegant style and humane manner. 'Trust in your fear of God. It is the sure guarantee of divine help,' he says to Job. 'This must now be your hope.' Then, as Job rejects this comfort and cries out anew in his misery, the second friend, Bildad the Shuhite, takes over. He pursues the thought of Eliphaz a bit further, even if he is somewhat sterner in his way of putting it, and begins to point out the specific consequences of this attitude. With him also there is certainty at the very outset:

> Does God pervert justice?
>   Or does the Almighty pervert the right?
> If your children have sinned against him,
>   he has delivered them into the power of their
>   transgression.
> If you will seek God
>   and make supplication to the Almighty,
> if you are pure and upright,
>   surely then he will rouse himself for you
>   and reward you with a rightful habitation. (Job 8.3–6)

And then again the key-word hope appears. It grows out of a similitude:

> Can papyrus grow where there is no marsh?
> Can reeds flourish where there is no water?
> While yet in flower and not cut down,
>   they wither before any other plant.
> Such are the paths of all who forget God;
>   the hope (*tiqwāh*) of the godless man shall perish.
>
> (Job 8.11–13)

What we now hear, incomparably more clearly than in the speech of Eliphaz, is this: 'Hope is present where a man is righteous. Where there is no righteousness, there are indeed grounds only for despair.'

Where this line of thought leads, this typical point of view of a devout wisdom that lives within a world of *maat*, of order, is finally made clear in the words of the third of the friends, Zophar the Naamathite. He openly demands righteousness of Job.

> If iniquity is in your hand, put it far away,
>   and let not wickedness dwell in your tents.
> Surely then you will lift up your face without blemish;
>   you will be secure and will not fear.
> You will forget your misery . . .
> And you will have confidence, because there is hope
>   (*tiqwāh*);
>   you will be protected and take your rest in safety . . .
> But the eyes of the wicked will fail;
>   all way of escape will be lost to them,
>   and their hope (*tiqwāh*) is to breathe their last.
>
> (Job 11.14–20)

One cannot miss hearing what is said to the stricken Job here: 'Hope is available to you. Be righteous, then you will have every reason for hope.'

How different, at first appearance how irreligious and even blasphemous the words of Job sound in response. They are, in the first place, the complaint of one who simply can go no further.

> What is my strength, that I should wait (*yḥl*) [hopefully?]
>   And what is my end, that I should be patient?
> Is my strength the strength of stones,
>   or is my flesh bronze? (Job 6.11f.)

Because any real hope has been stripped from him, he can now only hope for death. This hope for death means, however, the bankruptcy of any real human hope.

> O that I might have my request,
> > and that God would grant my desire (*tiqwāh*);
> that it would please God to crush me,
> > that he would let loose his hand and cut me off. (Job 6.8f.)

Of his life Job knows only: 'My days are swifter than a weaver's shuttle, and come to their end without hope (*tiqwāh*)' (Job 7.6). With mournful bitterness Job compares man to the tree. Whereas it holds for man that:

> Man that is born of a woman
> > is of few days, and full of trouble.
> He comes forth like a flower, and withers;
> > he flees like a shadow, and continues not,

it can be said of the tree:

> For there is hope (*tiqwāh*) for a tree,
> > if it be cut down, that it will sprout again,
> > and that its shoots will not cease.
> Though its root grow old in the earth,
> > and its stump die in the ground,
> > yet at the scent of water it will bud
> > and put forth branches like a young plant.
> > > (Job 14.1f., 7ff.)

The uncanny thing here lies in the fact that these statements are not statements about an event experienced fatalistically, but it is precisely in these things, precisely in this smashing of all hope, that God himself is active.

> The waters wear away the stones;
> > the torrents wash away the soil of the earth;
> so thou destroyest the hope (*tiqwāh*) of man.
> Thou prevailest for ever against him, and he passes . . .[3]
> > > (Job 14.19f.)

The weird thing here is this 'Thou' in the word addressed to God. Or later in the words in the third person:

> He breaks me down on every side, and I am gone,
> > and my hope (*tiqwāh*) he has pulled up like a tree.
> > > (Job 19.10)

In the great concluding speech of Job, which gathers everything up and leads into the challenge of God, we hear again:

> I cry to thee and thou dost not answer me;
> I stand, and thou dost not heed me . . .
> But when I looked (*qwh*) for good, evil came;
> and when I waited (*yḥl*) for light, darkness came.
>
> (Job 30.20, 26)

What has happened to Job here? He is thoroughly in accord with the opinion of his friends that hope can only come from God. He argues passionately against them, however, as they insist on the basis of their conception of order that man by his conduct has a share in this dispensing of hope by God. Out of his situation of utter ruin he holds fast to the conviction that although he has been pious by all human standards, God has nevertheless struck all hope from his hands and there is no possibility that his piety can win hope back for him.

To the devout mentality it appears as though Job's discourse here is truly blasphemous, evil, and impious. This in any event is how his friends understand his speech, and their horror rises more and more as he talks. So the surprise is all the greater when at the end of the book of Job we hear from the mouth of God himself, when he appears in the storm, the word that Job, although he is struck dumb with fright before the omnipotence of the Creator and must lay his hand over his mouth, has spoken more correctly than his friends (Job 42.7). How are we to understand this? The meaning evidently is that Job, with his admittedly quarrelsome and disputatious speeches about the freedom of God who will not be tied down to any system that can be manipulated by human conduct, recognizes the truth about the living God more profoundly than his friends do. In his speech, no matter how rebellious and impious it may have sounded at first, he has given God honour quite other than his wise and pious friends, whose speeches were meant to defend God.

At this point we must also take a look at Ecclesiastes.[6] Only in one place, where the Septuagint renders the Hebrew *biṭṭāḥon* (trust) by *elpis* (hope), does he expressly deal with the problem of hope. Eccles. 9.1ff. refers to the fact that all human life on earth has the same destiny. Death is the all-powerful leveller. In this connection the Preacher says: 'But he who is joined with all the living has hope (*biṭṭāḥon*), for a living dog is better than a dead lion' (v. 4). If we next ask whether the hope of the living is really any advantage, any 'plus', we hear first (v. 5) the sarcastic answer: 'For the living know that they will die, but the dead know nothing.' But from v. 7 comes the exhortation to enjoy what is given in the present:

Go, eat your bread with enjoyment, and drink your wine with a merry heart; for God has already approved what you do. . . . Enjoy life with the wife whom you love, all the days of your vain life which he has given you under the sun.

It is clear both here and at other points that even when he concentrates on the 'given' of the moment, the Preacher gives God the glory and honours him as the giver of all that the day brings to hand, or as he himself says, he 'fears God'.

This attitude is also clear in Eccles. 3.10f., where the word 'hope' is not expressly present, but where we are clearly dealing with the problem of the future and the possibility of man taking hold of the future. Here first is the word that God has set eternity in the heart of man. This word has been much puzzled over. I believe that in this word there is the thought that man finds himself compelled to press beyond and think beyond the simple present. In this pressing beyond, which the Preacher sees as a peculiar quality of human life, given to man by God, one sees instinctively the 'image of God' of Gen. 1, of which we will speak more fully later. And we easily recognize in the desire to secure a promise of security for tomorrow man's hunger for hope. The ability to prognosticate suggests the possibility of firm expectations and hopes that have some basis. But the Preacher continues this discussion with the statement that man cannot discover, cannot comprehend from beginning to end the work that God is doing. Here is the clear assertion that the future belongs to God alone. There is no truly certain prognosis that is able to take possession of tomorrow. Thus the train of thought returns to the present and to the admonition to take hold of the good that is given with the present.

I know that there is nothing better for them than to be happy and enjoy themselves as long as they live; also that it is God's gift to man that every one should eat and drink and take pleasure in all his toil. (3.12f.)

But the shaping of the whole course of events – and that means also the shaping of the morrow not yet knowable to man – is a matter of God's own eternal decision. 'Nothing can be added to it, nor anything taken from it; God has made it so, in order that men should fear before him.' (3.14).

The Preacher is related to Job in that he also fully recognizes God's unfettered lordship over what happens in the world. But whereas he, in a strikingly self-critical attitude of resignation, gives himself up to enjoy what is given in the present, there is in Job beyond this the passionate longing to discover yet something more of the future and of hope. Behind this longing there is in Job the knowledge that God the Creator will yet have something to do with his creation – an undoubtedly genuine Old Testament conviction that never comes to expression with the Preacher, proving him to be a marginal figure in the Old Testament. But if God really desires to have dealings with man, as Job knows he does, then there must yet be hope even for a Job, even for a man deep in the night of tribulation.

I think that it is from this perspective that we are to understand four statements of Job's which we must now discuss. They are statements that lead strangely near to the edge of the utopian, to that which is really the unthinkable. There is the despairing statement in Job 13.13–16:

> Let me have silence, and I will speak,
>   and let come on me what may.
> I will take my flesh in my teeth
>   and put my life in my hand.
> Behold, he will slay me; I wait upon him [hope in him? – *yḥl*][7]
>   yet I will defend my ways to his face.
> This will be my salvation,
>   that a godless man shall not come before him.

In a desperate breakthrough toward the future Job dares to put himself in a situation where he is threatened by death: he challenges God. If God should allow this, then there is still a glimmer of salvation for Job, in his waiting – his hoping? His wish in 14.13–15 sounds strangely unreal:

> O that thou wouldest hide me in Sheol,
>   that thou wouldest conceal me until thy wrath be past,
>   that thou wouldest appoint me a set time, and remember me. . . .
>   All the days of my service I would wait (hopeful waiting, *yḥl*)
>   till my release should come.

Thou wouldest call, and I would answer thee;
  thou wouldest long for the work of thy hands.

In his distress Job sits in the midst of Sheol, in the underworld. His words affirm this distress. He does not cry out for deliverance from his trouble. But he shapes an impossible desire, that God might shelter him even down there in that completely god-forsaken place, until the time of wrath is past – formulates the audacious thought that after this time of wrath God will again long for his creature and call him back to himself. But this would mean a new future, an all-embracing hope.

In 16.18f. and 19.25 we have two instances of legal terminology which Job employs as he attempts to formulate a possible hope. Out of a faith which is expressed also in the story of Cain, the faith that the blood of a murdered man does not remain concealed, does not come to rest even in the grave but cries out and so prevents a simple *causa finita*, Job cries,

O earth, cover not my blood
  and let my cry find no resting place.
Even now, behold, my witness is in heaven,
  and he that vouches for me is on high.
My friends scorn me;
  my eye pours out tears to God,
that he would maintain the right of a man with God,
  like that of a man with his neighbour. (Job 16.18f.)

Hope is not expressly mentioned here, but behind these words stands Job's knowledge that God has once said 'yes' to his right to life and that his friends' argument, their denial of his right to life before God on the basis of their cold conception of the order of things, is a lie. For this conviction Job has a witness in heaven, even God himself. And he appeals to this God against the God of hopelessness, the caricature of God that his friends hold up before him. He pleads, therefore, that his blood might not be covered up, might not cease to cry, because the question of justice would be dismissed if there were no longer a cry, the 'cry of murder', calling for justice. He will yet have his day in court. And the God whose 'yes' he is certain of, the same God who will again yearn for his creature, will intervene and make clear his right to life, step in as his witness.

If in Job 16, God is viewed as a witness, then in Job 19 the juridical figure of the redeemer is used. In a tribe where blood has been spilled and someone murdered, the *go'ēl,* redeemer or blood avenger, has as the nearest relative the task of demanding an accounting in blood, the death of another, thus on the basis of tribal justice achieving justice by compensation. When Job says in Job 19.25, 'For I know that my *go'ēl* [that is, my redeemer] lives and a guarantor [literally 'another', which must be a legal term here also: a substitute, who steps in where the first man can no longer manage] for me stands upon the earth', we must be clear that this is said by one whose blood has already been poured out, who is already dead. But even in death he knows that there is someone who stands up for his right even then and who will see to it that this is acknowledged again. Here we are dealing with the question of Job's right to life before God, a right that remains certain in no other way than through God himself, a right which the friends of Job do not acknowledge, and which God's wrathful dealings with Job, his pursuit of him even to death, do not reveal. Whatever world-view may be implicit in these statements is not spelled out. It would be false to speak here about a doctrine of resurrection and eternal life. For our purposes it is significant only in that Job, in the midst of all his despairing complaints about his revived life and lost hope, confesses that in God himself – for the sake of God himself – there are yet latent possibilities. For his own sake, in that as he has acknowledged his creature, he has as the Creator of man made himself in law the relative of man. This is not understood as a right which man can command by means of his own activity, nor as a hope that he has claim on by virtue of his own endurance, as in the conception of a world order which Job's friends have made into fixed dogma, but rather it is understood as a hope that remains with God alone because he is God and as such cannot betray his own promise.

By this route, leading as it does from the Proverbs by way of Ecclesiastes and Job through the crisis of hopeful faith into the ultimate depths of reflection about hope, we discover the peculiarly decisive character of Old Testament hope. According to the Old Testament faith, hope is only legitimate where God remains the sole Lord, in activity, in gift and in promise, and where man anticipates the future in no other way than as the free gift of God. Wherever human hope is propped up by means of a neutral world-view or some conception of world order, wherever it is ultimately dependent upon a solely human attitude, however deeply pious it may be, it is built on shaky ground and will one day in a crisis break up like that house that is built upon the sand.

NOTES

[1] H. Gese, *Lehre und Wirklichkeit in der alten Weisheit. Studien zu den Sprüchen Salomos und zu dem Buche Hiob* (Tübingen 1958); 'Les Sagesses du Proche-Orient ancien', *Colloque de Strasbourg, 17–19 May 1962* (Bibliothèque des Centres d'études supérieures spécialisés, Paris 1963).

[2] H. Ringgren, *Sprüche* (ATD 16², 1967), pp. 1–122; B. Gemser, *Sprüche Salomos* (HAT 16², 1963); W. McKane, *Proverbs* (OTL, 1970).

[3] H. Brunner, *Altägyptische Erziehung* (Wiesbaden 1957).

[4] Cf. e.g. Gese, *op. cit.*

[5] A. Weiser, *Das Buch Hiob* (ATD 13⁵, 1968); G. Fohrer, *Das Buch Hiob* (KAT, 1963). Cf. also J. Hempel, 'Das theologische Problem des Hiob', *ZST* 6 (1929), pp. 621–89 (=*Apoxysmata*, BZAW 81, 1961, pp. 114–73).

[6] W. Zimmerli, *Das Buch des Predigers Salomo* (ATD 16², 1967), pp. 123–253; K. Galling, *Der Prediger* (HAT 18, 1940), pp. 47–90; H. W. Hertzberg, *Der Prediger* (KAT 17⁴, 1963).

[7] This reading is to be preferred to the Hebrew: 'I wait not'.

III

STATEMENTS ABOUT HOPE IN THE PSALMS

IN the wisdom literature of the Old Testament the whole realm of reflection about man and his world was opened up. The focus of that reflection was not speculative research into the ultimate causes and forces of reality, as with the Ionian pre-Socratic philosophies, but the question of the practical mastery of life's realities seen in the totality of the world. In these writings this reflection is confronted with the phenomenon of hope. Here the question of the possibility of hope is posed in all its rigour as the writers of Ecclesiastes and Job find themselves unable in their collision with the mystery of the reality of the world to settle for the schematizations at hand.

We now turn to the Psalms, the prayer-book for the worship of the Old Testament congregation. Because we are dealing here with the words which were used by Old Testament man, and by the community to which he belonged, to approach God, we anticipate from the outset that the phenomenon of hope will find expression here. Man's question about his future and the possibility of life in a perilous present must inevitably emerge wherever he opens his mouth to call upon his God.

First a few preliminary words about the Psalms. The one hundred and fifty songs gathered here by no means represent a homogeneous collection all belonging to the same species. Research in the Psalms, in which the names of Gunkel, Mowinckel, and Westermann[1] denote the various stages of recent form-critical work, has made clear what a variety is brought together here in one collection. The Hebrew name of the song book, *tehillim*, 'Songs of praise', a word associated with the verb used in the call to praise, *hallelujah* – 'praise Yahweh', underlines even in the title that aspect of the Psalms in which the praise of God is richly represented. The term 'song of praise', as in Westermann, is preferable to the term 'hymn' used by Gunkel. The 'song of praise' is a species of song that finds its proper home in the congregation, even as, for example, the appeal to the worshippers in the call *hallelujah* makes clear. It can only be the song of the individual in a derivative and translated fashion by being transformed into an appeal to oneself: 'Praise Yahweh, my soul.' After the call to praise a main section ordinarily follows in which the call to praise is substantiated by reference to the mighty acts of God in creation and history. The derivative sense in which Zion, the city of God, can also become the object of praise need only be mentioned in passing here.

But the main division of the songs in the Psalter, in spite of the Hebrew title 'Collection of Songs of Praise', represents not the praise of God, but the group of songs that arise out of the other basic movement of man's prayer life, the petition. The song of petition, called in Gunkel's terminology a 'song of lamentation', belongs on the basis of form criticism to the wider group, the 'song of thanksgiving', which in its turn is related to the song of praise; it also belongs to the 'song of confidence'. In the song of lamentation man cries out to God in the midst of his tribulation. The song of thanksgiving, which Westermann designates more precisely as a 'narrative song of praise' and includes with the songs of praise, looks back on past trouble, often in such a way that the lamentation spoken in the midst of that trouble is repeated word for word. Here God is thanked for the help granted. In the song of confidence the element of trust, which again and again appears in the song of lamentation, here takes shape as an independent song form.

As a third group we can point to the wisdom psalms, in which the element of meditation stands out strongly and which are very similar to the wisdom literature in attitude, as we will shortly demonstrate by examples.

If we wish to be complete, we should identify another smaller group of psalms – namely the royal songs, a designation which many now extend to include among others the pilgrim songs. But as our interest lies primarily in the expressions of hope and expectation of the future in the Psalms, it is not necessary to extend the categorization any further.

In dealing with the question of hope and the future in the Psalms, we do well, in the light of the material we considered in the preceding chapter, to begin with the wisdom psalms. Let us therefore

begin with a brief look at the first psalm of the entire Psalter. Psalm
1 is presented as a prologue to the whole psalter and seeks to make
clear at the very outset a certain way of understanding it. The fact
that several textual witnesses to Acts 13.33 identify a quotation
from Ps. 2 in the Psalms as we have them as a quotation from Ps. 1,
indicates that the introductory psalm occasionally was not counted
as one of the psalms in the numbering of the 150. This introductory psalm presents two types of men: on the one hand the one

> who walks not in the counsel of the wicked,
> nor stands in the way of sinners,
> nor sits in the seat of scoffers,
> but his delight is in the law [instruction] of Yahweh,
> and on his law [his instruction] he meditates day and night,

and on the other hand the 'godless'. With images partly found in
the Egyptian 'Instruction of Amen-em-opet'[2] with its antithesis of
the 'heated man of a temple' (that is, one who is hot headed, impudent, foolish) and the 'truly silent', that is the wise, and which
reappear in modified form in the wisdom sayings of Jer. 17.5–8,
the devout man is here compared with the 'tree planted by streams
of water, that yields its fruit in its season, and its leaf does not
wither', and the wicked with 'the chaff which the wind drives
away'. The word 'hope' or 'to hope' is not present here, but there
is no mistaking what these pictures intend: the righteous man who
avoids evil and meditates on the law of Yahweh day and night has
a future. This is not described as a mere phenomenon of the
calendar, an empty future time, but it is filled with content. It is
the authentic future of fruit-bearing. And in the same way with
the image of the scattered chaff the wicked are not characterized
with the mere absence of future years of life, but with the nothing-
ness and fruitlessness of life which has no real future. To this extent we are confronted here too in other words and images with
the possibility of hope in human life and the absence of such hope.

This description of the two types of men and the possibility or
impossibility of hope that stands before them, reminds us indeed
of the conclusions reached in the conversation of Job with his
friends. We only hear this Psalm aright when we recognize that
in it the future and prosperity and fruitfulness come solely from
the hands of God and are not just possibilities that lie in man's
path and at his disposal. On the other hand only when it is realized

that, because hope comes only from God, the godless are therefore on a path that offers no promise or future – only when the psalm is heard in a way that leaves all freedom to give or withhold with God and acknowledges that it is his free gift that never leaves those who hold to him and his word of direction – only then does this psalm escape the verdict that is pronounced on Job's friends in the book of Job.

The same observation can be made about the statements in Ps. 37 where hope is expressly mentioned. This wisdom psalm with its sections gives the impression of successive rows of proverb-type sentences exactly as one might find in Proverbs. It has the art form – not particularly poetic to our taste – of an acrostic poem. The initial letters of each of the 22 couplets go through the alphabet. Two couplets which are close to one another in meaning, 8f. and 34, speak of a hopeful waiting upon Yahweh. The former bases its admonition that we ought not to hanker jealously after the good fortune of the godless on the assertion:

> For the wicked shall be cut off;
>> but those who wait (*qwh*) for Yahweh shall possess the land,

whereas v. 34 admonishes us:

Wait (*qwh*) for Yahweh, and keep to his way [that is, the way commanded by him],
 and he will exalt you to possess the land;
 you will look on the destruction of the wicked.

The dangerous proximity to the theology of the friends of Job cannot be overlooked. Only as the thought of waiting upon Yahweh here also remains completely open toward God and therefore knows that God's free faithfulness will give the land to his own (there is an echo here of the memory of the grant to Israel long ago of a share of the promised land), only then can the sentence stand up before the insight won in the words of Job.

An enormous acrostic psalm (Luther called it the 'golden ABC') is found in the psalter as Ps. 119. In it no less than eight single statements begin with the same letter of the alphabet, so that with its eight times twenty-two (=176) verses, it is far longer than any other psalm. The peculiarity of this psalm, to which A. Deissler has devoted a monograph of over three hundred pages,[3] consists in the fact that here the concept of the word of God, a concept which includes pre-eminently the revelation of God's commands, advice, and precepts, occupies the central place. It is not a God beyond history, surmised from his words in nature, that is presented here, but a God who has graciously disclosed himself to his people. It is toward this self-disclosure, then, that a hope is directed which is referred to in the psalm no less than eight times (*yḥl* six times, *śbr* twice; in 119. 95 *qwh* is used in a secular sense to refer to the stealthy waiting of an enemy). The psalm is often dismissed as a legalistic psalm attributable to the late faith of a congealed legalism. But even so, a careful scrutiny of the psalm at this very point reveals just how much the 'word of God' as understood here first opens man up to that which is to come and makes him a creature of expectation.

> Remember thy word to thy servant,
>   in which thou hast made me hope (*yḥl*). (v. 49)

The psalmist knows that the divine word promises help:

> My soul languishes for thy salvation;
>   I hope (wait – *yḥl*) in thy word. (v. 81, cf. v. 166 where *śbr* is used)

And therefore he knows complete assurance even as he waits:

> Thou art my hiding place and my shield;
>   I hope (*yḥl*) in thy word. (v. 114)

The waiting is repeatedly transformed into a cry:

> Uphold me according to thy promise, that I may live,
>   and let me not be put to shame in my hope (*śēber*). (v. 116)

> I rise before dawn and cry for help;
>   I hope (*yḥl*) in thy words. (v. 147)

It might almost appear from this that the word itself is what may be expected from the future. In one instance, however, the (apparently already revealed) commandment takes the place of the word:

> And take not the word of truth utterly out of my mouth,
>   for my hope is in thy ordinances. (v. 43)

So this demonstrates, on the contrary, that nothing less than the word that speaks to man and already guides him today is the word that at the same time opens him up to the future, awakes expectation and promises help. In astounding fashion the psalm affirms at one point that the presence of one who waits upon God's word means joy for the whole congregation:

> Those who fear thee shall see me and rejoice,
> because I have hoped (*yḥl*) in thy word. (v. 74)

Here the seclusion of the expectant man in the realm of his own private piety is broken. As the word, whose coming the Old Testament faith affirms, is not a private word to the individual, so the gamble of hope in God remains not a private experience, but one which serves to build up the whole congregation.

It has surely become clear that in spite of any recognizable elements of wisdom literature, Ps. 119 has begun to leave behind the sphere of an observing and reflective wisdom. Therefore it is time to take up the psalms in which a hopeful waiting comes directly to expression. This is found among the songs of lamentation (=songs of petition) and the related psalms of thanksgiving and confidence.

When a man lives in quiet peaceful circumstances and has all that he outwardly needs, he will as a rule talk less about hope than when he is cast into utter extremity and inner and outer temptation and when everything becomes overwhelmingly uncertain. Here he is confronted unavoidably with the question as to whether this danger means that he is lost or whether he still has a future and something to anticipate in this future. Here the problem is expressed in his words and questioning. This situation of temptation and distress is the place where the lamentation psalm has its own setting in life. The question dealt with in Job in relation to wisdom, and which becomes an issue in the conversation with the friends as a kind of argument about their experience of life, finds expression also in Israel's worship as the sufferer brings his petition to God in the sanctuary. Thus in Ps. 69 as the speaker lifts his voice to cry in his despair:

> Save me, O God!
> For the waters have come up to my neck,

immediately thereafter (v. 3) the agony of waiting is portrayed:

> I am weary with my crying;
> my throat is parched.
> My eyes grow dim
> with waiting (*yḥl*) for my God.

Here too we recognize the speaker's consciousness that he experiences his suffering not only as an individual but as a member of the congregation of those who share with him the experience of hope as he prays:

> Let not those who hope (*qwh*) in thee be put to shame through me,
>   O Lord God of hosts;
> let not those who seek thee be brought to dishonour through me,
>   O God of Israel. (v. 6)

Waiting on God is described in the parallel sentence as a seeking
after God. At the same time there is something else that becomes
evident here as the speaker later says:

> I looked for pity, but there was none;
>   and for comforters, but I found none. (v. 20)

Side by side with his waiting upon God there appears a waiting
for human comfort. This would surely be misconstrued if we took
it to mean rejection of waiting upon God, an expression of hope
and reliance upon man as the real guarantee of hope. These comforters too are to be seen within the setting of the congregation.
Part of the comfort would be that alongside the afflicted ones
appear men who, in the solidarity of the same hope in God, are
able to give genuine comfort. This was the essence of Job's anguish, that his friends apparently came as such comforters, but, as
we learn from his own lips in 16.2, proved to be 'miserable comforters' as they held before him a caricature of God instead of real
hope in the living God.

If we examine one by one the individual places in the psalms of
lamentation in which hope (waiting) is expressly mentioned, it becomes apparent that these expressions are found most often in the
so-called confessions of trust to which the one who prays is led
and with which he substantiates his own cry to God. Thus in the
acrostic psalm of lamentation, Ps. 25, we hear the worshipper say,
after an introductory petition for God's help: 'Let none that wait
(*qwh*) for thee be put to shame' (v. 3); somewhat later he substantiates another request with the expression:

> For thou art the God of my salvation;
>   for thee I wait (*qwh*) all the day long. (v. 5; cf. also v. 21)

In the cry and complaint of the one who utters Ps. 38, he feels the
anger of God upon him, is struck down with illness and is beyond
hearing and speech, but then he bursts forth with:

> But for thee, Yahweh, do I wait;
>   It is thou, O Lord my God, who wilt answer. (v. 15)

It is even more surprising to hear in Ps. 71, a prayer by one oppressed by the troubles of age, first the word of confession:

> For thou, Lord Yahweh, art my hope (*tiqwāh*),
>> my trust from my youth, (v. 5)

and then a word about the manner in which this waiting takes place, at least so far as its content is concerned:

> But I will hope (*yḥl*) continually
>> and will praise thee yet more and more. (v. 14)

Here we learn that hope gives God the honour. In that it entrusts everything to him and expects everything from him, it praises him as the real Lord of life. The confession of faith in the psalm of lamentation can also express itself in an imperative form. The conclusion of Ps. 27:

> Wait (*qwh*) for the Lord,
>> be strong, and let your heart take courage;
>> yea, wait (*qwh*) for the Lord,

should be understood not as the benediction of a third party,[4] but as the self-exhortation of the worshipper, with which he ends his supplication. The form of such an exhortation, which can also be directed toward the entire congregation, is found in the penitential Ps. 130, 'Out of the depths I cry to thee, O Lord'. After the worshipper, calling on God out of the depths of affliction because of his sin, has described his waiting and hoping:

> I wait (*qwh*) for Yahweh, my soul waits (*qwh*),
>> and in his word I hope (*yḥl*);
>> my soul waits for the Lord
>> more than watchmen (wait) for the morning (Ps. 130.5f.)

he then summons the congregation:

> O Israel, hope (*yḥl*) in Yahweh!
>> For with Yahweh there is steadfast love (covenant grace),
>> and with him is plenteous redemption (v. 7)

Especially impressive is the speaker's self-admonition to wait, as it is found in the threefold refrain of Pss. 42–43, a strophic poem mistakenly divided into two parts. The psalm arose out of the special distress of the worshipper, who must live far from the temple of Jerusalem, in a strange land in which he encounters hostility, and who longs for the worship in Jerusalem, the common celebration of the congregation. Three times it is expressed in the refrain:

> Why are you cast down, O my soul,
>   and why are you disquieted within me?
> Hope in God; for I shall again praise him,
>   my help and my God.

After an introductory question of puzzlement directed inward toward himself, there follows the self-encouragement to hope, grounded in a positive reference to the coming day on which the praise of God will once again be fully expressed. When we ask about the content of the psalmist's hope, we get the impressive answer: It is not the elimination of momentary afflictions that is central, not the wish for a peaceful life, but the hope that he may one day come again to that place where God will be praised in the congregation. If we ask him further whence comes his certainty that this hope will find fulfilment, there is no clear-cut answer to be heard. It does appear, however, that his remembrance of the worship he had earlier shared in the temple constitutes the peculiar motive for his watchful certainty. What he once encountered as from God constitutes the secret guarantee that God will not leave him in the lurch. God does not let fall any work that he has begun. We meet this affirmation again in different words in Paul's writings, in the introduction to Philippians (1.6).

After the strong grounding of expressions of hope in the expressions of trust found in the psalms of lamentation, it is not difficult to understand that this expression of hope is found also in the independent songs of faith. The refrain in Ps. 62.1,

> For God alone my soul waits in silence;
>   from him comes my salvation,

is varied in the repetition in v. 5,

> For God alone my soul waits in silence,
>   for my hope (*tiqwāh*) is from him.

In Ps. 131 the movement is from the beautiful picture of the psalmist's trust in God, portrayed in the reference to a child quieted at its mother's breast, to the summons:

> O Israel, hope (*yḥl*) in Yahweh
>   from this time forth and for evermore. (v. 3)

For the hope of Israel has no time limit.

In the same way we hear in the song of thanksgiving, which looks back on trouble survived, the word telling how hope in God has proven itself meaningful. In the narrative part of his song of thanksgiving, the one who has been heard, who brings his thank-offering to the temple, reports:

> I waited patiently for Yahweh;
>   he inclined to me and heard my cry.
> He drew me up from the desolate pit,
>   out of the miry bog,
> and set my feet upon a rock. (Ps. 40.1f.)

Here the writer dares to formulate a firm statement of faith that holds true beyond the moment:

For the needy shall not always be forgotten,
  and the hope (*tikwāh*) of the poor shall not perish for ever. (Ps. 9.18)

At the conclusion of Ps. 31 the group of friends and relatives invited to the thank-offering are clearly included in the admonition to wait on God. The word which the worshipper in the song of lamentation, Ps. 27, uttered in self-encouragement, here embraces the entire group present at the sacrifice as it gathers to express gratitude for the deliverance from trouble:

> Be strong, and let your heart take courage,
>   all you who wait for Yahweh (v. 14).

If the transmitted text of the thanksgiving festival song, Ps. 52, is in order, then another variation of the formulation becomes recognizable:

> I will thank thee for ever,
>   because thou hast done it.
> I will proclaim [wait upon – *qwh*] thy name, for it is good,
>   in the presence of the godly. (v. 9)

In place of hope in Yahweh we have here hope in the name of Yahweh. In the name, in which in some measure the revealed, approachable side of God is presented, the whole reality of God as it is directed toward man can be seen again and again in the Old Testament. Thus it is possible to speak of hope in the name. However the text at this point does not appear to be too certain, so one ought not to lay too much weight on this.

Next to the statements about human hope in the songs of lamentation and their form-critical circle, there are the scanty contributions of those hymns which Westermann, with terminology reminiscent of Gunkel, designates as 'descriptive Songs of Praise' and which have less significance in content also. In Ps. 146.5 the man who is praised because he expects help from the God of Jacob, is described in the parallel statement as a man whose hope (*śēber*) rests in Yahweh, his God. Again in Ps. 33, in which the loving-kindness of God is praised, those who fear the Lord are identified in the parallel statement of v. 18 as 'those who hope (*yḥl*) in his steadfast love'. Verse 20 confesses:

> Our soul waits (*ḥqh*) for Yahweh;
> he is our help and shield.

And the final verse 22, in which the song leaves the basic style of a hymn to become a petition, says:

> Let thy steadfast love, Yahweh, be upon us,
> even as we hope (*yḥl*) in thee.

Similarly Ps. 147.11 can also affirm in its praise of God:

> But Yahweh takes pleasure in those who fear him,
> in those who hope (*yḥl*) in his steadfast love.

In contrast to these, a statement with its own special character is the one found in Pss. 104.27 and 145.15, in which the creature, even the animal world, waits (*śbr*) for Yahweh 'to give them their food in due season'. The thought that all creatures are dependent upon the creator is expressed also in Akhenaton's 'Hymn to the Aton', which is strikingly related to Ps. 104, and even before this in the Egyptian 'Hymn to Amun-Re'.[5] It seems to be characteristic of the Old Testament that in this connection too hopeful waiting is introduced. The thought of hope here undergoes in this one particular instance a remarkable expansion to include the breadth of all creation – all of which is faintly reminiscent of Job. If we now survey the psalmist's statements about human hope and faith in the future, two conclusions stand out with special vividness. The first is the observation that all serious hope in God, that is to be helpful in life, is concentrated upon the one God of Israel who is called upon with the name of Yahweh. In contrast to Israel's polytheistic surroundings there is no other besides him toward whom

man can look. Nor is there any other way in which man can obtain
hope for himself. If it was ever said that the sufferer waited (hoped)
for human beings who would come and bring comfort, even so
there was clearly no thought of their comfort as a substitute for
waiting upon God, but rather as the very timely help that a fellow
man could offer in the form of comfort even in this waiting upon
God. But in addition to this there is a second conclusion: we are
struck by the decisive certainty with which the psalmists speak of
the help that lies in Yahweh for the believer. If we think back
again to the statements of the book of Job, they might appear to be
in almost direct contradiction to this. If there the voice of a radical
criticism of hope was heard, then the Psalms are penetrated with
an impressive certainty about hope. The question must be raised
as to the basis for this certainty about hope. The suspicion might
well arise that here man is again propping up his hope with some
kind of fixed world-view based on definite data available to him.

In the light of this question it is helpful to look a little more
closely at Ps. 39. It is a psalm that speaks out of deep distress, and
at first reminds one with its dark tones of Job's critique of hope.
The psalmist confesses at the outset that he had intended to keep
his interior distress to himself and not put it in words. But then he
can no longer contain the burning fire within him. So now he must
speak. He spreads before God the oppressive agony of his nothing-
ness and mortality:

> Yahweh, let me know my end,
>   and what is the measure of my days;
>   let me know how fleeting my life is! (v. 4)

It seems that he is compelled to unfold a picture of the world that
is without hope or future.

> For I am thy passing guest,
>   a sojourner, like all my fathers.
> Look away from me, that I may know gladness,
>   before I depart and be no more! (vv. 12b–13)

In this view of human life there is no existential hope to be found.
It sounds the more surprising then, when in the middle of this
agonized exposition in which the psalmist begs God for the
resignation appropriate to this point of view, we hear quite unexpectedly,

>And now, Lord, for what do I wait (*qwh*)?
>My hope (*toḥelet*) is in thee.
>Deliver me from all my transgressions.
>Make me not the scorn of the fool! (vv. 7f.)

Where is there detectable in this psalm any sign of a view of the world that provides support for hope? In terms of his view of the world the psalmist stands right where Job stood. But out of an existence from which there is no exit he reaches out for God with a tenacity even beyond that of Job's, and lays all its troubles before his feet, the affliction of his guilt, his distress at the words of those who jeer at him in his trouble.

>Remove thy stroke from me; . . .
>When thou dost chasten man with rebukes for sin,
>   thou dost consume like a moth what is dear to him;
>   surely every man is a mere breath! (vv. 10f.)

How is it that he ventures on a hopeful grasping after God when there is no substantiation by way of a world-view to which he can appeal to change his fate – a complete contrast to the speeches of the friends of Job?

In this connection we must also look at ch. 3 of the so-called Lamentations of Jeremiah.[6] The five songs found in the little book of Lamentations are not to be thought of as from Jeremiah. These are songs, four of them in acrostic form, in the style of psalms of lamentation, but distinctive in that they are occasioned by anguish over the destruction of Jerusalem. And in Lam. 3.18–29 we are clearly confronted with the question of the possibility of hope. In v. 18 the lamentation begins far down in the depths with the confession,

>So I say, 'Gone is my glory,
>   and my expectation (*toḥelet*) from Yahweh.'

But then in v. 21 it reaches a surprising conclusion:

>But this I call to mind,
>   and therefore I have hope (*yḥl*):
>The steadfast love of Yahweh never ceases,
>   his mercies never come to an end;
>they are new every morning;
>   great is thy faithfulness.
>'Yahweh is my portion,' say my soul,
>   'therefore I will hope (*yḥl*) in him.'

> Yahweh is good to those who wait (*qwh*) for him,
>   to the soul that seeks him.
> It is good that one should wait (*yḥl*) quietly
>   for the salvation of Yahweh.
> It is good for a man that he bear
>   the yoke in his youth.
> Let him sit alone in silence
>   when he has laid it on him;
>   let him put his mouth in the dust –
>   there may yet be hope; . . . (*tiqwāh*)

And then the hope is expressed that Yahweh will not be eternally angry but out of the riches of his grace will show mercy. It is difficult to overlook how close this is to Job's utopian wish that God might preserve him in the underworld until the time of wrath is past; only here the note of hope is struck with incomparably more certainty. At the same time it is clear that there is in no sense any support for this hope derived from the power of any system of thought. The 'perhaps' of the last statement of hope speaks clearly enough to this point with its reference to the complete freedom of Yahweh, upon whose decision alone the fulfilment of hope rests. In connection with this appeal to Yahweh himself and his freedom, there emerges here also mention of that covenant grace which is always capable of renewal. This is the basis for the audacious statement: 'Yahweh is my portion.'

Behind the mention of 'portion' stands the event of the allotment of the land, in which the participants each received their lot. From tribal history we know that according to the later tribal enumeration one tribe remained without a share of the land. But in explanation of this remarkable situation we learn that Yahweh declares himself to be the lot of this tribe of Levi, which then becomes in consequence the special priestly tribe. So it may be that behind this formula, which is used here and elsewhere as a pious expression that has nothing to do with the tribal distribution of the land, there exists an originally levitical form of speech. But the question that still lies behind our example runs like this: How can it be that a man in the hour of his deepest depression, in which he first confesses that his hope in Yahweh has foundered, and in which he subsequently does not even dare to go beyond 'perhaps' – how does it happen that this same man is able to take hold of a statement of such certainty as 'Yahweh is my portion'? And behind this question lies the even deeper one: 'On what basis is a real hope ventured here?'

At the conclusion of this discussion of the Psalms we ought to consider yet another psalm from the Psalter, one which does not, to be sure, contain the word hope, but whose hope, nevertheless, ventures beyond that of any other psalm. As regards type, Ps. 73 is considered one of the wisdom psalms, in which one of the problems of life is considered. Here the problem is that encountered again and again in the wisdom literature, the good fortune of the godless. In an account expressed in very personal terms, the psalmist describes his distress over this question and the offence that the well-being of the godless gives him, so that he himself has come close to deserting God. But then comes the turning point. In an expression which unfortunately cannot be completely clarified as to precise content, the psalmist confesses that his tribulations continued 'until I went into the sanctuary of God; then I perceived their end' (v. 17). Are we to think here of a particular experience in the sanctuary in which he is impressed by the truth proclaimed there? Or are sanctuaries spoken of metaphorically, as referring to the holy mysteries of God which the psalmist has managed to fathom? However the change may have come about, it is clear in any case that one who was up to this point deeply troubled now acknowledges God with a positively terrifying certainty:

Nevertheless I am continually with thee;
　　thou dost hold my right hand.
Thou dost guide me with thy counsel,
　　and afterward thou wilt receive me to glory.
Whom have I in heaven but thee?
　　And there is nothing upon earth that I desire besides thee.
My flesh and my heart may fail,
　　but God is the strength of my heart and my portion for ever. (vv. 23–26)

Again we encounter this determined laying hold on certainty: 'God is my portion!' And because this is so, then nothing can ever shake the certainty that the psalmist has a future with this God, he will lead him, and will finally even transport him into glory.

These last statements reveal a penetration of areas which are by no means opened up, let alone mastered on the basis of a world-view. All the certainty of this thrust rests in the conviction: 'Yahweh is my portion.' It is this that contains all the hope and confidence in a certain future. What Job dares to assert about the 'redeemer' (also entering into completely unexplored areas), is present here in the knowledge that 'God is my portion'. Where God in this way makes himself man's portion, death is no longer able to thwart the hope of one who is so held by God.

The Psalms present us with sentences of audacious certainty which are not substantiated further but are ventured as affirmations of faith. Now our next task must be to take a look at the other Old Testament expressions in order to determine whether there also we encounter such certainty and whether we cannot there finally discover something of the foundations upon which such confident cleaving to God grows. The close restriction to word usage, which guided us through the world of the wisdom literature and the Psalms, will now be given up, and we shall now enquire about the substance and content of hope and of the future.

NOTES

[1] H. Gunkel and J. Begrich, *Einleitung in die Psalmen. Die Gattungen der religiösen Lyrik Israels* (Göttingen 1933); H. Gunkel, *Die Psalmen* (Göttinger Handkommentar zum Alten Testament II.2⁴, Göttingen 1926); S. Mowinckel, *Psalmenstudien* 1–6 (Videnskapsselskapets Skrifter II, Hist.-filos. Klasse, Kristiania, 1921–24); id., *The Psalms in Israel's Worship* I–II (Oxford 1962); C. Westermann, *Das Loben Gottes in den Psalmen* (Berlin 1953); also particular investigations in C. Westermann, *Forschung am Alten Testament* (ThB 24, 1964). Cf. also A. Weiser, *The Psalms* (ET of 5th ed., OTL, 1962); H. J. Kraus, *Psalmen* (BKAT 15², 2 vols., 1961).

[2] Text in J. B. Pritchard, *Ancient Near Eastern Texts relating to the Old Testament* (Princeton 1950), pp.420–25.

[3] A. Deissler, *Psalm 119 (118) und seine Theologie* (Munich 1955).

[4] Cf. e.g. Kraus *ad loc.*

[5] Pritchard, *op. cit.,* pp.369–71 and 365–7.

[6] A. Weiser, *Klagelieder* (ATD 16², 1967), pp.295–370; W. Rudolph, *Die Klagelieder* (KAT 17.3, 1962); H. J. Kraus, *Klagelieder (Threni)* (BKAT 20, 1956).

IV

MAN AND HIS HOPE
ACCORDING TO THE YAHWIST WRITER

IN our passage through the Old Testament statements to this point we have allowed ourselves to be guided by the actual word for this phenomenon of 'hope'. This led us in the area of the poetry of the psalms of the Old Testament to very confident statements about hope. In any event the same thing that had emerged so clearly in the statements of Job with their criticism of hope became apparent in the framework of the Psalms. Hope cannot seriously be spoken of as though it were a possibility humanly inspired or produced. But the place where man encounters his creator and Lord is where hope lies. In contrast to both Ecclesiastes and Job, the Psalms dare to speak copiously of the hope which actually opens up to man in God. In the light of this state of affairs the question arises how the psalmists could speak with such certainty (beyond that of Job) concerning the hope that opens up to man in God. How can one who knows so certainly that God is not at man's disposal, as is the case not only with Job, but also, for example, with the worshipper of Ps. 39 – how can such a one speak so unexpectedly and definitely and with such deep conviction about God as the Lord who is present for man? So it is now in order, with greater freedom from simple questions of word usage, to ask about the basis of Old Testament faith in Yahweh. On what does this faith base its conviction that its hope will not be destroyed?

The kernel of the Old Testament, which has also retained the position of greatest respect in the reading in the synagogue, is the Torah, the complex of the five books of Moses. The history of the canon reveals that from this core the entire Old Testament subsequently came into being. Next to the Torah come first the 'Prophets' which include in the Hebrew canon the historical books of history from Joshua to II Kings as well as the prophets in the stricter sense (excluding Daniel). As a further step in the growth of the Old Testament the remaining writings of the Old Testament were gathered together under the loose heading 'writings'. So it ought to be the proper approach to begin our inquiry with the innermost core of the Torah, asking what it says about God and the possibility of a hope opening up to man in God.

The first thing that strikes us when we come to the Torah with this question is that we are not dealing here with academic instruction of a general nature about the relationship of God and man. Rather are we confronted from the very first sentences with a narrative that relates how God has dealt with the world and with man and what course this history has subsequently taken. In this narrative abstract conceptualization is at a minimum. Rather do we have here a description of the way in which, through the ages, things happen in the encounter of God and man. The relationship between God and man must be inferred from these events.

Then we notice a second thing. If we follow with a critical and attentive ear the story related in the book of Genesis, we soon are aware that we are hearing not a single voice, but a number of narratives woven together. At the beginning, where the prehistory of mankind is reported, we recognize two characteristically distinctive narratives to which more material has subsequently been added. So in what follows we are concerned with listening to the statements of both of these important narratives presented as from the beginning.

It is wise to begin with the older of the two narratives. We have grown accustomed to identifying the author as the Yahwist. This name is derived from the special viewpoint of this strand of the narrative. In it God is spoken of quite naturally from the very beginning by the name of Yahweh. It is clear that the later narrator, the so-called priestly writer, represents in this matter a characteristically different point of view. We must just make one point about the identification of the Yahwist as the 'author' of the narratives that take their name from him. Investigation has made clear that with the Yahwist we are not dealing with an author in the modern sense, the 'author' of a literary work who freely shapes and sets down his work. Rather, the Yahwist is bound to a body of tradition previously known and occasionally already firmly contoured which he does not simply reshape again. But it surely does not reflect the content correctly to speak of the Yahwist as a mere collector of traditions. We can clearly recognize the reshaping intention, betrayed not only by the selection of available material but also in the placing of very decided emphasis and the occasional insertion of sections formulated quite independently. The general design of the Yahwist is governed by a very definite declaratory intention. This justifies scrutinizing his narrative, for the definition of which I rely in large part on the analysis of M. Noth,[1] in spite of the complexity of the questions the Yahwist poses on individual points, with regard to the general question of his statements about a foundation for hope in Old Testament faith generally.[2]

The Yahwist begins his narrative with the primitive history of the whole of mankind. One can trace here quite clearly how he takes up the tales that have come down to him and how their fusion into a continuous spread of narrative does not quite come off. But on the other hand one can also see how these rather unwieldy traditions are held together in an over-all statement by a determined purpose and are made, each with its own material, to serve this general statement.

The narrative of the Yahwist, which, as we have it now, is preceded by the priestly account of the creation with its seven days, begins in Gen. 2.4b with an initial superscription that reminds one of the beginning of 1.1. 'In the day that "Yahweh God" made the earth and the heavens.' After a brief description of the initial and primitive condition of desolation, in which nothing yet existed and in which a mist formed, we come directly to the first expressly reported creative act of God, the creation of man. 'Then "Yahweh God" formed man of dust from the ground, and breathed into his nostrils the breath of life; and man became a living being.' The perspective from which the Yahwist reports the story of the world's beginning is completely recognizable. He is not concerned with the cosmos or the world-order but from the very outset with man, the real creation of God.

Then it goes on to report how God endowed this man. He plants a glorious garden. Behind this picture we can see without difficulty the old mythical tradition of the garden of God. He sets man down in this garden, gives him a task, and hands over to him the riches of the fruit of this garden – the desert dweller's longing and dream. Then he considers what more he might do for man.

God's deliberation with himself, 'It is not good that the man should be alone; I will make him a helper fit for him' (Gen. 2.18), betrays to the listening ear his purpose to prepare his very best for man. So God creates the animal world in the hope that it will be a help to man. And as it becomes clear with the naming of the animals, which man is empowered to do himself, that they are not the help intended for man by God, then he creates the woman as a being of man's own flesh and bone to stand beside him – a creature that the man immediately and joyfully recognizes as belonging to him, and to which he gives his own name. 'This at last is bone of my bones and flesh of my flesh; she shall be called Woman (*'iššāh*), because she was taken out of Man (*'iš*)' (Gen. 2.23). So here at the very outset is a description of the way in which God creates good for man.

In all this there is no explicit word about hope and the future of man. As in a dim reflection, however, there can be seen in the command of Gen. 2.17 what possibilities for man's hope and future are latent in what God in his goodness has done for man (if only man remains wholly bound to the giver of good). Of all the trees in the garden, man may eat of his own free will.

But of the tree of the knowledge of good and evil [it is possible that originally the text spoke only of a 'tree in the middle of the garden'] you shall not eat, for in the day that you eat of it you shall die. (Gen. 2.17)

In man's restraint before the one tree in the middle of the garden, his restraint before the giver, the one from whose hand he lives and has received everything, is meant to be kept alive. If man should allow himself to forget the giver behind the gift and thus reach for the fruit that, as forbidden fruit, is a reminder of the giver, then hope and future would be obliterated. For death is obliteration of the future and so also of any human hope. But if man remains obedient before his God (so one can see in retrospect) then his life remains full of future and hope. But here Gen. 3 takes up its account of man. First, in that yet another voice begins to speak between man and God, the voice of the tempter which sounds from the snake. The snake is not to be understood metaphysically, as though now beside God a second principle of the universe confronts man and man is seen as a poor creature at the mercy of two fundamental world powers. Rather the voice of the tempter arises out of the created world: 'Now the serpent was more subtle than any other wild creature that Yahweh God had made,' says v. 1, insisting here that the serpent too belongs wholly to the category of the created. Whatever the preceding stages of development of the narrative according to studies in the history of traditions, there is here stated, without any metaphysical dimensions, the mystery that there exists in the created world temptation which afflicts man and whispers into his ear a word that is irreconcilable with the will of the Creator: 'You will not die. For God knows that when you eat of it (the fruit of the tree) your eyes will be opened, and you will be like God, knowing good and evil' (Gen. 3.4f.). But this would mean for man complete power over his future: power to be as God, to know everything. Good and evil should not be construed narrowly here as meaning only knowledge of morality. This is intended as a double-barrelled expression that embraces opposite poles – the whole – everything. To know everything. And this means the ability to make every possible prognosis correctly and so have power over one's life even as the Creator himself has power over the whole of life. When subsequently we hear that the woman was full of desire as she looked at the tree, not only because the fruit appeared beautiful to the eye, but also because it was desirable to make her wise, we should note that the Hebrew word *haśkîl* used here is the word employed by the wise man to refer to his intelligence and capacity to cope with life. The story at all times asks the man who hears it, whether he does not recognize in his own human ways this other voice of the will to self-mastery over life and future, the desire to be as God.

The story then goes on to tell how man gives in to this voice and in so doing loses his real future. In the curse that God speaks upon the man who succumbs to this voice, the loss of future and hope comes to full expression. For the woman it means pain in childbirth and submission to him to whom she feels herself drawn. For man it means servitude to the weariness of labour and death:

In the sweat of your face you shall eat bread till you return to the ground, for out of it you were taken; you are dust, and to dust you shall return.
(Gen. 3.19)

Here there stands before us the man who is sketched so clearly in the statements critical of hope in Job and Ecclesiastes. 'Man that is born of woman is of few days, and full of trouble. He comes forth like a flower, and withers; he flees like a shadow, and continues

not,' we read in Job 14.1f. And the words of Ecclesiastes, as
we may well remember from the first of Brahms' 'Four Serious
Songs', are:

For the fate of the sons of men and the fate of beasts is the same; as one
dies, so dies the other. They all have the same breath. . . . All go to one
place; all are from the dust, and all turn to dust again. (Eccles. 3.19f.)

The only difference is that Gen. 3 goes beyond Job and Ecclesiastes in locating the thorn in man's experience in the fact that as
he grasps insolently after a hope and a future he can manipulate
autocratically, he frivolously rejects the future made possible by
the creator.

Whoever listens carefully then to the Yahwist's story of the Fall
and the curse in the garden of God and the expulsion that neces-
sarily follows (according to a more markedly mythological variation, an expulsion from the place where the tree of life stands),
will easily hear something else also. 'In the day that you eat of it
you shall die' sound the forbidding words of God before the tree.
'In pain you shall bring forth children,' runs the curse over the
woman (Gen. 3.16). Bear children? This would then be a future,
living on in a coming generation. When the narrative near the end
goes on to say that the man gave his wife the name *ḥawwāh* (Eve)
because 'She was the mother of all living' (Gen. 3.20), it makes
apparent how man under the affliction of the curse which drives
him away from life, nevertheless grasps for that hidden promise
in which God with apparent inconsistency still holds out a prospect of a future and of life, holds on to man even in his sin, and
directs his attention toward that which is to come.

The fact that we have not missed the mark with such an understanding of Gen. 3 is demonstrated by the story which the Yahwist
tells immediately thereafter in Gen. 4, the story of Cain's murder of
his brother. Immediately upon man's impudent grasp at what God
has reserved for himself, there follows the story of the first pair of
brothers in which brother murders brother and man forfeits his
right to life once again. For the Old Testament law in Ex. 21.12, in
wording reminiscent of the command of God in his garden, says:
'Whoever strikes a man so that he dies shall be put to death.'
Cain's life – and that means also his future and his hope – is therefore subject to death. But it is striking that at the conclusion of
this narrative, in which Cain, filled with anxiety before the curse of

God upon him, says: 'Whoever finds me will slay me' (Gen. 4.14),
there appears again something of the mysterious inconsistency of
the divine mercy, which kills and yet does not kill. God takes
Cain, who is driven from his presence, a wandering fugitive who
will never again know a home, under his own personal protection,
marks him on the forehead with his own sign, (not the 'mark of
Cain' of which we commonly speak as of the mark of a curse, but a
mark of protection) 'lest any who came upon him should kill him'
(Gen. 4.15).

And this development continues in the narrative of the Yahwist.
In an awkward tradition, which appears never to be fully in con-
trol of its mythological material, Gen. 6.1–4 reports that the sons of
God – an Old Testament expression for angelic beings in the
service of God – go in to the daughters of men, and that giants –
the Greek world talks here of heroes – are born of these marriages.
Because of this disruption of the proper order of the world, God
limits the ultimate age of man to 120 years. But the Yahwist con-
spicuously concludes here with the story of the great flood, which
is supposed to cleanse the sinful nature of man.

Yahweh saw that the wickedness of man was great in the earth, and that
every imagination of the thoughts of his heart was only evil continually.
And the Lord was sorry that he had made man on the earth, and it
grieved him to his heart. (Gen. 6.5f.)

So there comes the great flood. But from this flood God, who had
just regretted even making man, prudently saves a whole family of
people, who will be able after the flood to continue the human
species – a renewal of the future just where all future appeared
wiped out under the threatening aspect of God's regret over the
creation of man. At the conclusion of the flood narrative the Yahwist, in deliberate repetition of the negative judgment upon man,
reports how God promises man and the world a future.

I will never again curse the ground because of man, for the imagination
of man's heart is evil from his youth; neither will I ever again destroy
every living creature as I have done. While the earth remains, seedtime
and harvest, cold and heat, summer and winter, day and night, shall not
cease. (Gen. 8.21f.)

This is how the Yahwist describes the primitive history of the
human species: subjected to death by his own guilt before God,

characterized by hopelessness, and yet in the midst of this ruin still sustained by God. One cannot say that in promising children to the woman, in protecting Cain from murder, in preserving the human race through the great flood, God is here writing over the world a great promise for coming life. But certainly this world is peculiarly protected – this we must say: but is this for something yet to come?

The continuation of the narrative makes clear that this is the understanding of the Yahwist. With Gen. 12 he turns from the world-wide story of mankind to the more exclusive history of the patriarchs of Israel. At this transition point the shaping hand of the Yahwist can be seen with special clarity.

Directly before the shift to the patriarchal narrative, unmistakably and intimately linked to this point in the story, the Yahwist relates the story of the Tower of Babel. Here again mankind as a whole is before our eyes. In the lowlands of Mesopotamia settlements had formed. Here the newly discovered technique of sun-dried brick construction had been used to build a city, and in this city a high tower whose top is supposed to reach to heaven. The motive for this undertaking is given in the two-part statement: 'Let us make a name for ourselves, lest we be scattered abroad upon the face of the whole earth.'

In this duality one can recognize the cry for a future and for hope. Dispersal over the world would mean danger. Clustering together allowed hope for preservation and future possibilities. In the 'name' that it seeks by building the tower, mankind grasps for life after death in posthumous glory, even as the mighty men of the world in every age have sought to guarantee eternity with their monuments.

Against the background of this event to which God responds with the dispersal of mankind, the Yahwist relates in Gen. 12.1–3, in an insertion that is unmistakably of his own composition, the beginning of the story of Abraham. Without any elucidatory introduction we hear that this man has encountered the living address and promise of Yahweh.

Go from your country and your kindred and your father's house to the land that I will show you. And I will make of you a great nation, and I will bless you and make your name great, so that you will be a blessing. I will bless those who bless you, and him who curses you I will curse; and by you all the families of the earth will bless themselves.

If a generation of city- and tower-builders believed in securing the future by determined accumulation of power and the clustering together of the masses, here is a single man called out of the sheltering environment of land, family, and kin and set defenceless upon a way that stands under the guidance of God alone. And while the people of Babel thought to make a name for themselves with the tower that touched heaven and so win eternity, this defenceless individual, led on his way by God alone, is here promised the name that will continue and that will receive the promise of a future.

But we have still said too little. The words spoken to Abraham make clear that this is not only the beginning of the history of a private individual, but with the journey of this individual, whose life has been seized by the divine promise, there begins simultaneously that event which involves 'all the families of the earth' and which brings blessing into a world which until now has been tragically cursed. The Yahwist wants to make clear by the shape of his narrative that here a turning point is reached. The persistence with which the key-word 'blessing – to bless' occurs no less than five times in both of the quoted verses is intended to ensure that we realize that here the shift from the curse upon the world to blessing upon it is taking place. If the curse had to do with death, and that means loss of future and hopelessness – the statements of Job allow for this terminological interpretation – then blessing should now have to do with life, future, and hope.

And this is in fact what can be observed in the further narrative of the Yahwist about Abraham, Isaac, and Jacob. Like a scarlet thread the promise runs through the whole subsequent history of the patriarchs, though certainly with variations in the individual formulations, and keeps the story moving, a movement which reaches toward coming fulfilment full of expectation and hope. Abraham wanders away from his homeland and reaches the place called Shechem in northern Palestine. Then, according to Gen. 12.7 Yahweh appears to him and says: 'To your descendants I will give this land.' As a sign of what he has heard, Abraham builds an altar there. After his separation from his nephew Lot, who upon Abraham's generous offer of a free choice had chosen the best share of the land, Yahweh appears to Abraham a second time in Bethel, according to Gen. 13.14ff., and promises him possession of the land. 'All the land which you see I will give to you and to your descendants for ever.' Abraham wanders further. According to the report in ch. 15 of a renewed encounter with God, personal progeny is promised to him as one until now childless, and once again the promise of the land is repeated. As they pitch their tents in the southern part of the land near Hebron, the promise is again given, this time, according to Gen. 18.1ff., through three men among whom Abraham entertains Yahweh himself without knowing it; they promise the birth of a son in the following year. This hopeful expectation is fulfilled, and the narrative is further developed in Gen. 24 where Abraham sends out his servant to secure a wife for his son, Isaac, with the words:

The Lord, the God of heaven, who took me from my father's house, and from the land of my birth, and who spoke to me and swore to me 'To your descendants I will give this land,' he will send his angel before you, and you shall take a wife for my son from there. (Gen. 24.7)

As he speaks, something of Abraham's characteristically solid certainty becomes visible, that certainty in which he sees his life opening toward the promised future, that certainty out of which he also dares to trust God for the solution of the specific dilemmas which lie before him. Waiting and hoping are not expressly mentioned, but there is a repetition of the word of divine promise on the basis of which Abraham makes his way into the future and maintains himself in a land far from his homeland.

After Abraham's death the word of divine promise is renewed to his son, Isaac, to whom Gen. 26.3 says: 'Sojourn in this land, and I will be with you and will bless you' (cf. also v. 24). The same word comes to Jacob as he has to flee from home as the result of his fraudulent theft of the blessing. Yahweh encounters him in Bethel and says to the fugitive who apparently is guilty of throwing away all his future:

I am Yahweh, the God of Abraham your Father and the God of Isaac; the land on which you lie I will give to you and to your descendants. And your descendants shall be [as numerous as] the dust of the earth. (Gen. 28. 13f.)

It is this word to which Jacob appeals as he turns homeward again from afar and sees before him the dangerous encounter with the brother whom he had once betrayed:

O God of my father Abraham and God of my father Isaac, who didst say to me, 'Return to your country and to your kindred, (that is, to Canaan) and I will do you good,' Deliver me, I pray thee, from the hand of my brother, from the hand of Esau, for I fear him, lest he come and slay us all, the mothers with the children. But thou didst say, 'I will do you good, and make your descendants as the sand of the sea, which cannot be numbered for multitude.' (Gen. 32.9, 11f.)

In all these instances where hope is not expressly mentioned, one can see clearly that the divine promise is the power on the basis of which the patriarchs dare to live their lives of hope. Thus Abraham in dispatching the servant gains the assurance that God will show him the way and enable him to fulfil his assignment. Thus Jacob in the hour of dark distress appeals to God on the basis of his word of promise that he would smooth the way to the promised goal.

With the beginning of the book of Exodus a remarkable change of scene has taken place. The patriarchs have disappeared, and their descendants have become a great people even as was promised. But it is immediately apparent that the impulse of orientation toward a promised future, the tense expectation of a coming salvation, has by no means ceased to be important. To the offspring of the patriarchs, who are forced to suffer in Egypt as slave labour in shameful bondage, Moses is sent with the task of leading them out. In a passage that was perhaps added as an elaboration to the Yahwist account, Yahweh speaks within the framework of this sending of Moses:

I have seen the affliction of my people who are in Egypt, and have heard their cry. . . . I have come down to deliver them out of the hand of the Egyptians and to bring them up out of that land to a good and broad land, a land flowing with milk and honey. (Ex. 3.7f., cf. also 3.17)

With these words the theme is sounded out that will now dominate all subsequent accounts of the remaining books of Moses. We hear again of people on the move, making for a goal. In place of the patriarchal families with their eyes on the fulfilment of the promise of offspring and settlement in the land, there is now the pilgrim people of God, preparing, under the promise of a land flowing with milk and honey, for an exodus, a going out (originally to be sure this expression suggested a curse). In the difficulties of the wilderness wanderings they are continually in danger of looking back, longing for the flesh pots of Egypt. Again and again they are called by Moses to trust in the divine promise of a new future in the land.

In his investigation of the prophetic expectation of redemption in the Old Testament, S. Herrmann,[3] in an introductory section which explores the presuppositions of the prophetic expectation, puts his finger quite correctly on the fact that, in this expectation of a land flowing with milk and honey, we are dealing from the standpoint of the history of traditions with a fully independent complex of tradition. This did not have its original life-setting in the same place as the expectations of the patriarchal stories and therefore manifests a thoroughly independent form linguistically. It is therefore even more impressive that in the whole of the Yahwist narrative as we have it before us, we find two such periods of waiting and hopeful watching one after the other. This reveals the fact that hope and waiting and entering into an opening future is one of the basic elements of Old Testament faith. But in the light of this second phase of wanderings toward a future not yet achieved we must assert with special emphasis that it is the divine promise that stands over all else as the prime mover. It is not the special qualities of the people of Israel, inclined by interior disposition to what is new, that causes them to look forward. In the Yahwist text of the story of the spies, after the spies have told the people still wandering in the wilderness something of their exploration of the land and the dangers there, we hear from the mouths of the people: 'Let us choose a captain and go back to Egypt' (Num. 14.4). This is the attitude of the people. But neither is the audacious initiative of Moses, with his liking for bold enterprises, to be identified as the driving force. The account of events in the wilderness presents much more realistically the weariness of this great man, who at one point would like to throw the whole task at the feet of God, as he says:

Why hast thou dealt ill with thy servant? And why have I not found favour in thy sight, that thou dost lay the burden of all this people upon me? Did I conceive all this people? Did I bring them forth, that thou shouldst say to me, 'Carry them in your bosom, as a nurse carries the sucking child. . . ?' I am not able to carry all this people alone, the burden is too heavy for me. (Num. 11.11f., 14)

The texts seek to bring out that the one thing which continually calls God's people to hope and causes them to be the pilgrim people of God – travelling toward his future – is the promise of Yahweh alone. This calls them forward, this alone makes hope possible.

One would expect that with the arrival in and possession of the land the tension would be relaxed and the goal of the history of the pilgrim people achieved. We unfortunately have very little certain knowledge about the conclusion of the Yahwist narrative material, which is available to us, of course, only in material combined with other sources. It is possible that the last identifiable section is found in Numbers, which is still concerned with the wilderness period. But here we must add a footnote about the sections that can be attributed to the Yahwist with some certainty. In Num. 22–24 there is an account of a particular threat to the people of Israel as they prepare to enter the land of Canaan. King Balak of Moab brings the famous seer Balaam from a distant land so that he may curse Israel. Behind this act lies the firm belief that such a man of God can determine future history with a word of blessing or curse. But what happens then is that Yahweh, who according to Israel's faith holds all power in his hands, reverses the seer's words. Instead of cursing, the seer blesses Israel as the people lie camped in the valley before his eyes. In the Yahwist part of the story the word of blessing is heard a second time:

> The oracle of Balaam the son of Beor,
>   the oracle of the man whose eye is opened,
> the oracle of him who hears the words of God
>   and knows the knowledge of the Most High,
> who sees the vision of the Almighty,
>   falling down, but having his eyes uncovered:
> I see him, but not now;
>   I behold him, but not nigh:
> a star shall come forth out of Jacob,
>   and a sceptre shall rise out of Israel;
> it shall crush the forehead of Moab,
>   and break down all the sons of Sheth. (Num. 24.15–17)

Here our view is directed far beyond the point in time in which those who come from Egypt possess the land where flows milk and honey, the land of Canaan. Our view is carried forward to the great coming king who will conquer the Moabites and, as is clear in the continuation of the passage just quoted, also the Edomites.

The view here is unquestionably directed toward David. A subsequent third period of hopeful expectation appears in this word which comes right at the end of the Yahwist narrative, in so far as we can detect it with any certainty.

A variety of considerations have led to the conclusion that the Yahwist is to be dated in the period shortly after David. The question then presents itself: is this the time in which all expectations and all hope have achieved their goals, in which faith can live wholly in the present and need no longer be expectant? Even if one is predisposed to accept it, one is still astounded at the determination with which the Yahwist narrator apparently subsumes under the tension of expectation the entire history of Israel previous to the time of David, from the great turning-point at the beginning of the time of the flood to the commencement of the time of blessing (Gen. 12.1–3). But if we think back to that great entrance of the time of blessing, we can note that next to the proclamation of a great posterity, a great name, and the land which God had promised, there was also the statement that through Abraham and the blessing upon him, blessing would extend to all peoples. According to H. W. Wolff this is indeed the essential statement of promise that comes to view in Gen. 12.2f. Should the time of David be understood as a time in which all these promises are fulfilled? Is it not conceivable that even from here a further waiting and hoping stretches out toward a yet unfulfilled future? The Yahwist has not given us an answer in the material that we can recognize as his.

But surely the other question presses heavily upon us: how is it that the Yahwist sets the whole of the story of the Pariarchs and the beginnings of Israel, as he tells it in the books of Moses, so decisively under the key-word of promise, and understands this history as a journey travelled in hope on the basis of the promise experienced? This question must be pursued further in the next chapter.

NOTES

[1] M. Noth, *Überlieferungsgeschichte des Pentateuch* (Stuttgart 1948).
[2] H. W. Wolff, 'Das Kerygma des Jahwisten', *EvTh* 24 (1964), pp. 75–98 (= *Gesammelte Studien zum Alten Testament*, ThB 22, 1964, pp. 345–73).
[3] S. Herrmann, *Die prophetischen Heilserwartungen im Alten Testament* (BWANT 5.5, 1965).

V

THE BASES FOR THE STRUCTURE OF HOPE
IN THE ANCIENT HISTORICAL NARRATIVES
OF ISRAEL:
THE PRIESTLY ACCOUNT

THE Yahwist historical account, originating as it does not long after the time of David, left us with the question: What is the explanation of the fact that the account of the history of Israel up to that point stands so unmistakably under a movement toward the future? It was with a promise from Yahweh that the Yahwist narrative of the patriarchs began. It made Abraham into a wanderer whose hopes were fixed on a promised future. And correspondingly the age of Moses began with the promise of Yahweh and brought a far from willing people to set out on the way to the promised land. And then on the way through the wilderness there was the yet more distant promise of a coming ruler. Although the point at which the Yahwist's work ends is no longer known with any certainty, the promise at the entry into the land in Gen. 12.2f. leads us to suspect that the narrator knows of a promise that extends even beyond the time of David, and which does not release the faith of Israel from the attitude of hope even in the time of David. But how did this peculiar kind of movement toward coming fulfilment originate?

In a lecture about the kingship of Yahweh given at the Oxford International Congress of Old Testament Studies in 1959, V. Maag[1] attempted an understanding of the 'on the move' character of Old Testament faith in God, the King, based on the sociological past of Israel as a nomadic people. I cannot pass over the opportunity to quote a passage from his exposition, which formulates this point of view especially well:

The nomad lives not in the cycle of seedtime and harvest, but in the world of migration. This is the world of here today, gone tomorrow, where everyone knows that his children will die in some place other than where the parents are buried. In the realm of transmigration the event is experienced as a movement forward, as a leaving behind. This God leads to a future that is not mere repetition and confirmation of the present, but is the goal of the events yet in process. The goal is what gives meaning to the wanderings and their trials; and the present decision to trust in the God who calls is interpenetrated by the future.

Here without a doubt we find delineated uncommonly aptly the texts which describe Yahweh, the God who leads into the future and the future-oriented attitude of his people. But does reference to the constitution of nomadic Israel alone suffice to explain the faith of a people that had become settled in a land and the peculiarities of its God? The Greek tribes also arise out of a period of folk-wanderings, and yet their belief when settled on the land bears completely different features. Further facts must be brought in to explain Israel. G. von Rad has taught us to see that at the heart of the Pentateuchal accounts, the essential point around which they crystallize, is the confession of the God who led Israel out of Egypt.[2] This is more than just a remembrance of a nomadic past and the God who once gave guidance there. Rather is it the case that here a very definite memory is made into an element of the proclamation of the God who worked in this event. Next to this event must stand also the figure who raised this historical memory to the dignity of a proclamation, that is, the praise of the unique Lord who through this event redeemed and guided them. The assertion that Moses, the man with the Egyptian name, was this figure, seems to me to be historically obvious.[3] But this means the passing on not only of the knowledge of a definite structure of divine activity, but also at the same time the demand for reverence and worship of the God to whom this event bears witness. All Israel's more distant memories are subsequently subjected to this one claim. What Israel otherwise knows as a revelation of God, the patriarchal history, is made to conform to this confessional element. The appearances of God to the patriarchs are understood as events which prepare for the leading of Israel to Canaan, which is made possible by the salvation event of the flight from Egypt. These are not just events that happen alongside of others, but rather all Israel's memories are caught up in the whole of the great movement along the way by which God had led his people, and, it is hoped, will go on leading even beyond the present. In all these events it is not a law of history that is seen at work, but the great acts of God who leads and who in these acts purposes to be honoured.

What we are stressing here can be made even clearer if we inquire about the way of speaking about the future and about hope found in the second great narrative strand of the Pentateuch.

The Yahwist account reports the events that preceded the history of Israel proper, from the creation of the world until the people led out of Egypt were on the brink of the possession of the land.

The identical span of events from the beginning of the world until just before the conquest of the land is also related by the priestly writer, who wrote centuries after the Yahwist and into whose work the Yahwist account was subsequently woven.

The priestly account is clearly a later retelling. To be sure we ought not to overlook the fact that a variety of new and not unimportant narrative material has been included – in the introductory story of creation and at other points. But in its main lines it follows the earlier narrative. In this development we can recognize, however, a conscious tautening of the narrative through omission of a variety of narrative material which appears to be less essential to the main lines of the story. Often the narrative pieces inserted are so scanty that we might very well ask whether the priestly writings should be considered a narrative work at all, or whether the laws inserted in the document are the only important items.

Hand in hand with this tautening there is a strong stress on caesuras or, more correctly, points at which the events which relate God and the world are condensed in a way which effects a kind of periodizing of history. It begins with the mighty prologue of the creation events. There are ten generations – here we can recognize a trace of the ancient eastern attitude to pre-history which we have met before – to the time of the great flood, through which the important covenant between God and Noah is consummated (Gen. 9). Over a chain of representatives of nine generations this continues until Abraham. If we may include him, we arrive here, through a slight change in the manner of calculation, at the number ten. Here also in Genesis 17 an important covenant agreement shapes a new beginning. And then, as a further figure, Moses steps forward. Next to the very full description of his call in Exodus 6, the emphasis here is above all upon the description of the events on the holy mountain. Granted, any talk of a covenant is expressly avoided. According to P, all that happens is quite simply the fulfilment of what had already been promised to Abraham.[4] But with the ordering of worship in the tent of meeting and the introduction of the sacrificial cultus, this event obviously takes on great weight and shapes a new epoch. The question has already been raised as to whether we do not see behind this stress on four great events in world history the historical schema of the four periods of world history as found in Dan. 2 and 7.

Another feature of general style is equally clear. In the accounts of the first two periods of world history, the priestly writing identifies God exclusively by the simple descriptive term *'elōhīm*, God. In the encounter with Abraham this God reveals himself with the new name *'ēl šaddāi*, whose translation as the 'almighty' is by no means certain. According to type this name is a pre-Israelite Canaanite designation for God which is subsequently and partially taken over as a predicate of the God of Israel. This designation for God is found most often in the Old Testament on the lips of the friends who converse with Job – a dialogue which, according to the statement of the book of Job itself, takes place beyond the boundaries of Israel. The proper name for God by which Israel knows its God and which is used by the Yahwist even at the beginning of human history without further explanation, the name Yahweh, is according to the priestly writings first revealed to Moses. In Ex. 6.2f. Yahweh presents himself to Moses with the words 'I am Yahweh', and adds to this the explanation, 'I appeared to Abraham, to Isaac, and to Jacob as *'ēl šaddāi*, but by my name Yahweh I did not make myself known to them.' This point of view, according to which the name Yahweh does not become the proper form of address for God until the events associated with Moses, is shared, as Ex. 3 demonstrates, by the written source that we have only in fragments, the so-called Elohist. It contains unquestionably good tradition. But this memory is built into the priestly writings only in a very reflective view of the history of revelation. Out of the undefined worship of the early period there arises the revelation of the God of the fathers under the name *'ēl šaddāi*. God first reveals his name to Moses (according to the faith of Israel, the only true name) as Yahweh. Thus in successive steps of revelation God gradually makes known his essential being. For name includes essence. But can we recognize – and we ask this now on the basis of our general theme – in this clearly progressive history of revelation, something of a disclosure of a future for man, a call to step out with hope toward what is coming?

At the beginning, in Gen. 1.1–2.4a, enclosed in the time-frame of the seven-day week, we find the great story of the creation of the world. What the Yahwist only touched on with a few broad strokes is here extensively developed. The construction of the cosmos, which according to the world-view of Gen. 2 emerged out of the unsubstantial beginning of an arid primal desert, is here conceived of as arising out of a watery chaos (the picture of the world as of a great alluvial plain with its yearly inundation), described here in great detail. Man appears for the first time not at the beginning, but rather at the end of the description of the beings created in the world. The broader cosmological interest distinguishes the priestly writing from the Yahwist with his immediate and direct interest in man.

But this does not mean that in the presentation of Genesis 1 man is unimportant. Together with the land animals he is created within the limits of the sixth day. But he is raised up over all animals in that he and only he is created after the image of God. Here a statement which was used originally only of a king (although in ancient Egypt it is also found democratized and used of ordinary men) is here used as the identifying characteristic of man. The account is further elaborated in that man is entrusted with 'dominion over the fish of the sea, and over the birds of the air, and over the cattle, and over all the earth and over every creeping thing that creeps upon the earth' (Gen. 1.26). This statement finds its echo in the words of Ps. 8 which in praising God also speaks of man with amazement at his exaltation in comparison with the mighty heavens:

> Yet thou hast made him a little less than *'elōhīm* [which
>   refers here to the beings of the divine world, the
>   angels,]
>   and dost crown him with glory and honour.
> Thou hast given him dominion over the works of thy hands;
>   thou hast put all things under his feet [that is,
>   subordinated all to him],
> all sheep and oxen,
>   and also the beasts of the field,

the birds of the air, and the fish of the sea,
whatever passes along the paths of the sea. (Ps.8.5–8)

We will pause here and ask: are we not here at the place where
man's future really opens to him and where he achieves authentic
humanity? Man, empowered by the Creator, yes, even com-
missioned by him to subdue the world. We moderns would speak
here not only of dominion over the animal world, but also dominion over the inorganic world and the possibility of man making
use of its laws. Is this not the point at which man's future really
opens up and from which he can step out full of hope and expectation toward ever newer horizons, overtaking the given and con-
quering the new? No doubt we are very near to the proposal of
Ernst Bloch who, without speaking of God as Creator, sees man
as the one being who is so open toward the future that he moves
toward his authentic definition. According to Ernst Bloch the real
Genesis lies not at the beginning but at the end of the human story
as it is destined to be shaped by man.[5] Here we find ourselves without a doubt also echoing a widespread modern understanding of
man: man's hope lies in the fact that he himself creates his world.

Now certainly one cannot disagree that man, according to
Gen. 1, is in fact empowered to turn toward the future on the basis
of the command to know the world and make it serve him. Yet
without a doubt it would be a tragic misunderstanding of Gen. 1,
if we were to close the circle here and assert that the creation story
of the priestly narrator, in its view of hope, leads to a picture of man
that sees him greatly increased in numbers (these words are preceded by 'be fruitful and multiply'), finally bringing the world
created by him to his feet and thus achieving his essential future
destiny. This would be to overlook the most essential element of
the priestly writer's description of creation.

The creation week which the priestly writer describes does not
end with the last working day but culminates in the seventh day
on which God rests and which becomes a peculiarly complete and
hallowed day through this rest of God. 'God blessed the seventh
day and hallowed it.' God had also blessed man and animals, em-
powering them to be fruitful. But according to the whole story of
the beginning, he hallowed only this special day on which apparently all activity gives place to the exalted rest of the Creator,
who alone is in view. If we are to speak of the goal and the hidden
relationships of the world and so also of man, who is a part of the

world and of the six days of work, we must not overlook this
relationship. Man, the culmination of the six days of work, is,
according to Gen. 1.1–2.4a, related by his important commission
to a world in which God has established his holiness.

In any event it is evident that initially not a word is said about
the availability of this holiness for man. The holiness exists. The
seventh day exists as that which is hallowed by God and so as
that period of time set apart as his special property, giving every
working week its peculiar goal. It exists initially as the secret of
God. The further account of the priestly writer makes clear that
with this secret a hidden expectation is introduced into the created
world, a secret that one day will be revealed to man.

But first the priestly writer tells of the epoch between the creation and the great flood. Here the creation which was good breaks
up in a frightening way. The thought which the Yahwist, with his
pronounced anthropological interest, develops in his elaborate
portrayal of the disobedience in the garden of Eden and the
fratricide within the first two brothers, is here simply stated in
terms of its consequences with a brief observation: 'Now the earth
was corrupt in God's sight, and the earth was filled with violence'
(Gen. 6.11). In unmistakable contradiction of the statement in
Gen. 1.31, 'And God saw everything that he had made, and behold,
it was very good', the priestly writer's dictum in Gen. 6.12 is: 'And
God saw the earth, and behold, it was corrupt.' The great flood
whose waters, once banished in the creation process to a place
above the firmament and under the circle of the earth, are again
poured out on the earth and threaten to plunge the cosmos back
into chaos – that pre-creation condition in which the earth was
sterile and empty – is God's answer to the corruption of the earth.
But then God himself again rescues the threatened world from
this fate, because he remembers Noah who is righteous in his sight.

He establishes a covenant with him which he confirms by hang-
ing his war-bow in the clouds, and he gives life to a world that had
developed darker features as a place of violence. The word hope
does not occur in Gen. 9, which speaks of this covenant. But what
this chapter says is that man, when he sees God's bow shining in
the heavens with the receding storm, may hear a promise through
this sign and may hope for a future and peace for his threatened
world. We hear very clearly at this point the word that hope for
the world after the flood does not depend on the world-conquering

capacities of man, but solely on the pledge given by God. On this pledge man can fix his faith.

Then with the introduction of the next epoch of world history, the priestly writer tells about the individual, Abraham. The graphic narrative about the call of Abraham in far-off Mesopotamia, about his wanderings and stopping-places, the call of God repeatedly spoken anew and the promise renewed again and again, all this disappears here. All that is significant between God and Abraham is compressed into the chapter about the covenant agreement between them (Gen. 17). Here God reveals his new name, '*ēl šaddāi*, to Abraham. Here he also gives Abraham, who until now had been called by the name Abram (this is also secondary material in the section by the Yahwist which precedes Gen. 17), his name Abraham, which makes clear the promise given to him: Abraham means, according to this explanation, 'Father of a multitude (of nations)'. Here also we find the promise that we have already met in the Yahwist account: The man who up to now is childless will be rich with descendants. The same thing is said of his wife, *šārai*, who now receives the name of *šārāh*, 'princess'.

This landless stranger passing through the land, shall possess it in his descendants, a land newly characterized now in an idealizing reflection as a 'land of sojournings'. To the two promises of the Yahwist tradition there is added now a third, which, as what follows will demonstrate, is especially characteristic of the priestly narrative: God on the basis of this covenant resolves to be the God of the descendants of Abraham:

And I will establish my covenant between me and you and your descendants after you throughout their generations for an everlasting covenant, to be God to you and to your descendants after you. (Gen. 17.7)

So God's promise calls Abraham once again to go forward into the future with hope. The threefold promise may well express a threefold hope.

After this only one other single scene from the Abraham story is related in detail, a scene that has no equivalent in the Yahwist's narrative, but which contains a peculiarly objective demonstration of the hopeful faith of Abraham. That the priestly writer, who is otherwise so sparing of narrative, develops this account so fully, is an important indication that this story, related apparently as a purely secular episode, nevertheless for him bears a weight of meaning.

Genesis 23 reports the death of Sarah. Abraham wishes to bury his wife. As a landless 'stranger and sojourner', as expressly stated in v. 4, he has no place that he can call his own where he can bury her. So we have the account of the wordy negotiations in which he deals with those who dwell in the land at Hebron in order to acquire a cave as a burial place of his own. Here it becomes very apparent that the proper acquisition of this cave before witnesses must be unconditionally secured. Abraham refuses simply to bury the dead in a grave of one of the inhabitants of the country, as is readily offered to him. In the same way he refuses simply to allow them to make him a present of the desired cave. But before the eyes of the Hittites who live there (it is underlined with great emphasis) he pays a not insignificant sum for the cave.

What is this detailed account of an apparently purely secular land-purchase supposed to mean? One can understand it properly in its entirety only when one has in mind the divine promise according to which this 'land of sojourning' is the land promised to Abraham. But he does not yet possess it. Nor dare he think of settling down there. Later the priestly writer will also report that the descendants of Abraham migrate to Egypt. But the dead, and this is what the account is trying to make clear with considerable emphasis, are not to be laid to rest in the graves of the residents of Canaan. The dead receive as a down-payment on the promise a piece of the land as their grave. Thus the priestly writer can further report with a care that appears almost pedantic that Abraham (Gen. 25.9), Isaac and Rebecca, Leah (Gen. 49.31), and Jacob (Gen. 50.12f.) are all buried there also. Jacob, dying in Egypt, begs his sons with great urgency to see to it that he also is buried there. Thus this grave is for the priestly writer an unmistakable allusion to the hope of the patriarchs. They own only a grave in the promised land. But by their stubborn insistence that their bodies be laid to rest in this grave in the promised land – not just anywhere – not down in Egypt as could well have happened in the case of Jacob – they witness to the promise established for them by the pledge of God, whose fulfilment they await in hope. The grave witnesses to the hope of the patriarchs. In this strangely objective form the priestly writer speaks of the liveliness of their hope. Further than that, he knows that after the death of Abraham God renews his promise to his descendants. Thus Gen. 35.11f. reports God's appearance and promise to Jacob at Bethel. In Gen. 48.4

Jacob recalls, as he elevates the sons of Joseph to the status of his own sons, a promise which also sounds in Gen. 28.3f., where Isaac blesses his sons.

But the memory of this promise is again present when, at the beginning of the next epoch in the priestly writer's story, God appears to Moses and commissions him to lead the descendants of Jacob, now a great people, out of Egypt, and bring them into the land promised to their fathers. No more need now be said about the promise of increase of descendants. Besides the promise of the land, which here as in the Yahwist provides the impetus for all that follows of the journey through the wilderness toward the goal, we again have fully expressed that third promise which in the priestly writings, in contrast with the Yahwist, appears for the first time:

I will redeem you with an outstretched arm and with great acts of judgment, and I will take you for my people and I will be your God; and you shall know that I am the Lord your God, who has brought you out from under the burdens of the Egyptians. (Ex. 6.6b–7)

Here new hope is awakened, hope of deliverance from present trouble and above all, even beyond this expectation, the hope that Yahweh will be God of his people and Israel will be his people.

With this we are prepared for the crucial point of the priestly version of the story of Moses: the encounter of God with his people on the holy mountain in the wilderness and the establishment of the cultus in the tent of meeting erected there. In this tent, on the basis of God's command, the place is to be established where Yahweh will be present in the midst of his people and thus wholly the God of his people, as he had already promised Abraham in Gen. 17. At the conclusion of the ordinances for regular sacrifice, we hear the pledge:

There I will meet with the people of Israel, and it shall be sanctified by my glory; I will consecrate the tent of meeting and the altar; Aaron also and his sons I will consecrate, to serve me as priests. And I will dwell among the people of Israel, and will be their God. And they shall know that I am the Lord their God, who brought them forth out of the land of Egypt that I might dwell among them; I am the Lord their God. (Ex. 29.43–46)

Then the following chapter describes how Yahweh, after the tent of meeting is established and the sacrifice is properly prepared, descends to meet with his people.

In this connection there is a further event: the mystery of holiness, hidden in God, according to the priestly writer, since the seventh day of the week of the creation, is now in the fulness of time revealed to the people for whom Yahweh had become God. This tradition in its details presents definite problems. On the one hand the story of the manna in Ex. 16 relates how the Israelites discover, from the fact that no manna falls on the seventh day, that the sabbath is the holy day of God. But there is also at the end of the regulations for the holy place of the tent of meeting in Ex. 31.12f. an explicit sabbath command:

You shall keep my sabbaths, for this is a sign between me and you throughout your generations, that you may know that I, the Lord, sanctify you.

In any case the priestly writer now clearly states that God allows man to share the blessed and holy possession of his rest. We should understand this to mean that God now sanctifies his people, that is, takes them to be his very personal possession. That which is intended for the world from creation itself, is proclaimed in and through the people of God, receives in them its public recognition. One could hardly express more strongly the importance of what comes to fulfilment in the time of Moses. But conversely it becomes clear that from this perspective the whole created world is now opened up toward that which until now remained hidden, but which is now disclosed to the people of God.

Before this mighty fulfilment of divine promise in which God in a visible order of worship becomes truly God of his people, the lively expectation of the Yahwist tradition toward a possession of the land recedes noticeably into the background. Whether the priestly writer says anything further of the ownership of the land is a matter of dispute.

Thinking back to the Yahwist, one would like to ask whether the promise of the coming king uttered by Balaam plays any further role here. In answer to this question one could look again at Gen. 17 where, in the framework of the promise to Sarah, we hear that kings of peoples will descend from her. But even this expectation, aroused within the setting of the covenant with Abraham, now recedes in importance before the tremendous event in which God becomes the God of his people.

Is it not the case then that the history narrated by the priestly writer loses its inner tension with the event at Sinai? Must it not follow from all this that the stress on hope as an element of the faith of Israel now fades in importance in the priestly writings as compared with its place in the Yahwist where history ever and again reaches forward to the future? Without a doubt the difference in the two forms of the narrative cannot be overlooked.

In comparison with the Yahwist the priestly writings tell the story with an emphasis characteristically their own. What they suggest even in the creation narrative with their concern with the 'holy', comes to light even more clearly later on: their peculiar concern is the glorification of the Lord, who as Lord not only stands over all creation, but appears again and again in the special history of the liberation and leadership of his people. As this Lord he desires recognition in the world in the mystery of his 'I', a mystery characterized by his name. Thus we hear at the call of Moses: 'You shall know that I am Yahweh your God, who has brought you out from under the burdens of the Egyptians.' So it is again in the priestly account of the fundamental event of Israel's credo, the wonderful departure from Egypt in the deliverance at the Red Sea – first as Yahweh announces the impending pursuit by the Egyptians: 'I will harden Pharaoh's heart, and he will pursue them and I will get glory over Pharaoh and all his host; and the Egyptians shall know that I am Yahweh' (Ex. 14.4). Then the identical sentence, slightly expanded, is repeated as the Egyptians, hard on the heels of Israel, are blindly led to venture onto the dangerous sea floor. The words from the mouth of Moses are very similar as he announces the wonderful feeding of the people with manna and quails:

At evening you shall know that it was Yahweh who brought you out of the land of Egypt, and in the morning you shall see the glory of Yahweh, because he has heard your murmurings. (Ex. 16.6f.)

And again immediately before the granting of the gift, from the mouth of Yahweh himself we hear:

At twilight you shall eat flesh, and in the morning you shall be filled with bread; then you shall know that I am Yahweh your God. (Ex. 16.12)

The same formula is heard as Yahweh promises to meet with his people in the holy tent.

And they shall know that I am Yahweh their God, who brought them
forth out of the land of Egypt that I might dwell among them; I am
Yahweh their God. (Ex. 29.46)

But now we must ask whether this appearance of Yahweh in
his self-glorification and this command to acknowledge his glorification has anything to do with the disclosure of a future and of
hope for man. This would hardly be the case if it was only a matter
of the glorification of God's self-sufficient majesty. But we can
recognize in the third pledge of God, newly added to the promise
to Abraham by the priestly writer, the fact that this writer is
especially conscious of the descent of this one glorious and holy
God to his people Israel. This is the reason for his historical narrative: to make the coming of Yahweh to his people visible. To
proclaim this is the main purpose of his account.

The priestly writer composed his narrative at the time of the
Babylonian exile. The story of the events which issue in the gracious approach of God to his people under Moses, is for him without
doubt not only a narrative written in retrospect about an ancient
'once upon a time'. Where God, the majestic, the creator of the
world and its foundations, condescends to his people and promises
himself to this people, we are not dealing with an aorist tense, but
rather with a perfect, yes, even with a future perfect. Here God,
the Lord of all time, pledges his word. But where he gives his
word, there is also a hope and a future.

In the priestly writings we are faced with another manner of
speaking about the hope and the future of the people of God. As
an analogy of the relationship of the Yahwist and priestly narratives, one is tempted to point to the relationship of the Synoptics
and John. In the former there is a narrative of particular events
and of the emergence of hope as Christ passes through these events.
In John there is very little movement, little striding through events,
but instead everywhere the majestic revelation of the glory of the
Son, that is, the revealer of the Father come near to man – but this
also, even if in a completely different way, impels hope, leads man
from today into tomorrow.

Here again we can return to what we said at the beginning of
this chapter. Referring to the nomadic background of Israel's
understanding of God, Maag has delineated the peculiar move-
ment-character of faith in Yahweh. Von Rad's reference to the
elements of proclamation in the remembrance of the Exodus from

Egypt and entrance into the land[6] brings sharply into focus the fact that in this narrative is expressed a faith in a Lord whose descent, manifest in his acts of guidance, makes evident his gracious lordship over his people. But both narratives – both the description of the way which Yahweh journeyed with his people, and the glorification of God's majesty – meant for Israel's faith the possibility of future, the disclosure of hope.

NOTES

[1] V. Maag, 'Malkut Jhwh', *Congress Volume, Oxford*, 1959 (SVT VII, 1960), pp. 129–53.

[2] G. von Rad, 'The Form-critical Problem of the Hexateuch', in *The Problem of the Hexateuch and Other Essays* (Edinburgh 1966), pp. 1–78.

[3] Cf. e.g. R. Smend, *Jahwekrieg und Stämmebund. Erwägungen zur ältesten Geschichte Israels* (FRLANT 84, 1963).

[4] W. Zimmerli, 'Sinaibund und Abrahambund. Ein Beitrag zum Verständnis der Priesterschrift', *TZ* 16 (1960), pp. 268–80 (=*Gottes Offenbarung*, ThB 19, 1963, pp. 205–16).

[5] Cf. in this connection ch. XI below.

[6] H. D. Preuss, *Jahweglaube und Zukunftserwartung*, understands the future expectation of Yahwistic belief distinctively on the basis of the Exodus proclamation.

VI

DEUTERONOMY
AND THE DEUTERONOMISTIC HISTORY

THE complex of the Torah, whose two most important narrative strands in the Yahwist and priestly writings we have examined on the basis of their proclamation of a future and a hope, closes in Deuteronomy with a major farewell speech by Moses. This speech contains in its middle section, chs. 12–26, a collection of commandments. According to the investigations of Noth,[1] this great speech in its present setting is the opening section of a historical account which, beginning with a backward look to the events during Israel's wanderings starting with the departure from Sinai, narrates the story of the possession of the land, and the periods of the judges and the kings, right up to the Judean exile in the neo-Babylonian period. Moreover, this historical work in its inner dynamic derives from the law-giving on Mount Sinai as unfolded in Deuteronomy. Noth has therefore identified it as a deuteronomistic historical work.

It falls to us now to give attention to the great speech of Deuteronomy, the sermon on the law, and the historical narrative deriving from it, and then to ask about the thought about the future and about hope found in both complexes.

It has long been observed that Deuteronomy, which we will discuss first, stands in a special relationship to the reform under Josiah, which according to II Kings 22 was sparked off by the discovery of Moses' book of the law. Even Jerome, in his commentary on Ezekiel 1.1, characterizes the time of Josiah as the time 'quando inventus est liber Deuteronomii in templo dei'. Since de Wette's *Dissertatio criticoexegetica qua Deuteronomium a prioribus Pentateuchi libris diversum, alius cuiusdam recentioris auctoris opus esse demonstratur* of 1805, the view has become firm that we must reckon with a special origin for this book of the law. The fact that the first

clearly tangible instance of its historical impact was Josiah's reform, led by a kind of mental short-circuit to the assumption that
this book of the law had its origin at approximately this same time
among the Jerusalem priests. According to this point of view these
priests, on the basis of the reform quickly created by this book,
consciously elevated their sanctuary to the place of central sanctuary of the land. Through a pious fraud they caused the unsus-
pecting King Josiah to play into their hands. Careful and detailed
investigations have more and more cut the ground from beneath
this thesis in more recent years. They have made it seem probable
that Deuteronomy arose among circles native to the traditions of
the northern kingdom, identified in the narrowest sense as Israel.[2]
The northern kingdom collapsed in the year 722 under the assaults
of the Assyrians. But its spiritual heritage did not go under, but
lived on after the destruction of the state. Even as the book of
Hosea, the prophet of the northern kingdom, subsequently attains
wider circulation in Judah, and also slight expansion by Judaic
hands, so it is also probable that Deuteronomy, originating after
722, finds its way to Judah and there has surprising impact in the
reform of Josiah in the hundred years after the destruction of
the northern kingdom. A closer look has further revealed that the
legal material of Deuteronomy has many counterparts in the
measurably older legal corpus of the 'Book of the Covenant' (Ex.
20.22–23.33).[3] This material in the first half of the core of Deuteronomy (chs. 12–26) has undergone a very characteristic reworking in which the concise legal sentences have been transformed
into broadly applied admonitions. This style of admonition also
ties the first half of the legal section to many sections of the introductory speech prefacing the law in Deut. 1–11, material which
arises out of the same circles. This is not the place to deal with the
complicated literary questions of this introductory section or the
concluding piece in chs. 27–30, which also may be considered
Deuteronomic in the narrower sense. It is clearly apparent that
various hands have worked on the whole complex of Deut. 1–30.
In individual passages the period after 587 can also be detected. In
any case the concern here is not with exposition of the individual
and varied parts of the legal material present here. Rather we
want to deal with the specific Deuteronomic theological framework, which holds together introduction, conclusion, and the
parenetically revised sections of law, from the perspective of

our overall question as to what it declares about hope and the future.

Deuteronomy introduces us to a definite historical situation. The people have concluded their forty years' wilderness wandering and stand on the far side of the Jordan ready to pass over Jordan into the Canaan promised to them. There in his great speech Moses imparts the Law of God to the people. It is presupposed here that these commandments have already been given to Moses on Mount Sinai, but that he has not yet passed them on to the people. For this the moment has just now arrived. Whoever might be inclined to wonder how it is possible that Moses could keep the commandments to himself so long, may find enlightenment in the superscription to the actual law section in 12.1 as to the way in which Deuteronomy itself understands this event. The speech of Moses to the people runs like this:

These are the statutes and ordinances which you shall be careful to do in the land which Yahweh, the God of thy fathers, has given thee to possess, all the days that you live upon the earth.

The break in style from second person plural to second person singular betrays the fact that the text has been subsequently clarified by an addition. It is a clarification that brings out in sharp relief what is to become the foundation of the admonition that follows: the point is that it is the law that is to be in force in the land of promise which the people are about to enter. In 6.1, in one of the introductory speeches, it is stated in a text without gloss:

Now this is the commandment, the statutes and the ordinances which Yahweh your God commanded me to teach you, that you may do them in the land to which you are going over, to possess it.

It is important that this formulation be correctly understood. It is not that Moses had not given the commandments of God until now because they are commandments that would first take on meaning in this new cultural setting after the passage of a nomadic people to a sedentary existence. The reference to the land has rather a meaning derived from its role in the history of salvation. With the gift of the land God makes good his ancient promise to the fathers, not only the patriarchs but also the fathers who escaped from Egypt. In this realm of promises fulfilled Israel is supposed to keep the commands that Moses now imparts. The response of the people to God in the keeping of the commandments is meant to be the response which will bring the people the full blessing of this new gift of salvation.

And if you will obey my commandments which I command you this day, to love Yahweh your God, and to serve him with all your heart and with all your soul, he will give the rain for your land in its season, the early rain and the later rain, that you may gather in your grain and your wine and your oil. (Deut. 11.13f.)

What awaits the people can be described with quite extravagant words:

For Yahweh your God is bringing you into a good land, a land of brooks of water, of fountains and springs, flowing forth in valleys and hills, a land of wheat and barley, of vines and fig trees and pomegranates, a land of olive trees and honey, and a land in which you will eat bread without scarcity, in which you will lack nothing, a land whose stones are iron, and out of whose hills you can dig copper. And you shall eat and be full, and you shall bless Yahweh your God for the good land he has given you. (Deut. 8.7–10)

And then there follows a further admonition to keep the commandments, not to become satisfied and thereby forget God.

Besides these clear and full statements which anticipate the attainment of the total salvation of the land and admonish obedience to the commandments on this basis, there are also other less clear formulations in which the final arrival in the land is connected with obedience to the commandments – as in 8.1:

All the commandment which I command you this day you shall be careful to do, that you may live and multiply and go in and possess the land which the Lord swore to give to your fathers.

But the main outlines of the message of Deuteronomy are not obliterated through this altered basis for obedience: the law proclaimed here by Moses directly before the entrance into the land is given to the people at a point where they have not only experienced great help in the past, but also stand directly before the overpowering fulfilment of the promise of salvation that God will accomplish out of love for the people he has called and out of faithfulness to the oath he swore to the fathers (7.8). In almost brusque words we hear in the introductory speech the word that by their behaviour the people have not really deserved such a redemption:

Not because of your righteousness or the uprightness of your heart are you going in to possess their land; . . . Know therefore, that Yahweh your God is not giving you this good land to possess because of your righteousness; for you are a stubborn people. (Deut. 9.5f.)

And then in 9.6f. they are reproached with their disobedience in the wilderness. The land is a free and undeserved gift, to which the people are now to respond with their obedience.

Now if we ask about the place hope and future have in this proclamation, we find we have really answered our question in what we have just said. According to Deuteronomy the people are standing on the threshold of the greatest possible blessing. They are entering into the realm of blessing opening before them, a realm of blessing they will preserve by their obedience.

The unusual theory about Deuteronomy is that here an entire legislative code is set within the sphere of immense hope and expectation. God's demand on the people does not stand there timeless, but is illuminated by the statement that a new future will be opened up for Israel. A people empowered with a great hope are here summoned to obedience to the commandments.

The future which the people are to enter is described in the words just quoted as a future that has the character of a gift. More can be said. In Deut. 12, at the beginning of the regulations, is found the so-called centralization law, that is, the demand that Israel shall recognize one place only for worship. In part of the preamble to this commandment in Deut. 12.8–10 we hear:

You shall not do according to all that we are doing here [outside the borders of the land] this day, every man doing [in his sacrificial worship] whatever is right in his own eyes, for you have not as yet come to the rest and to the inheritance which Yahweh your God gives you. But when you go over the Jordan, and live in the land which Yahweh your God gives you to inherit, and when he gives you rest from all your enemies round about, so that you live in safety. . . .

Again in Deut. 25.19 the future which Israel faces is described with the sentence:

Therefore when Yahweh your God has given you rest from all your enemies round about, in the land which Yahweh your God gives you for an inheritance to possess. . . .

As part of the future promised to the people, there is to be 'rest', peace with Israel's enemies.

If we evaluate Deuteronomy against the background of what we saw in the Yahwist account, we must come to the conclusion that the statements made there in which Israel is called to enter hopefully into the future through the promises of God, also turn up here quite unexpectedly and dominate the very different realm of commandment and instruction. This people called upon to hope is here summoned to obedience toward fully developed commandments.

Now we must look squarely at another question raised not long ago. In his Zürich lecture on the understanding of history in Deuteronomy,[4] H. H. Schmid, after placing the promise-element in Deuteronomy within the framework of the fiction of a speech by Moses at the time of the entrance into the land, points out that this book in reality is addressed to the people at the time of Josiah, that is, to a people who have dwelt in the land for a long time.

What in the fiction was future is now (specifically for the ears of the hearers actually addressed in the time of Josiah) present. And what in the fiction was a function of the future, must now be realized in the present: it must open up a future for the hearer . . . and Israel's future lies in maintaining a relationship with its present. The whole history of salvation which the fiction of Deuteronomy outlines is summed up in the present.[5] . . . Any essential historical advancement, the original pre-exilic sections of Deuteronomy do not anticipate. The possession of the land, that is, the present, is the culmination of the history of salvation. Thus it is possible – with reservations – to speak of a realized eschatology as essential to a factual understanding of Deuteronomy.[6]

Then Schmid asserts quite correctly that the promise heard in Deuteronomy exceeds the concrete reality of even the best of times in Israel. But this prolepsis of the promise is not, according to Schmid, to be understood as temporal, but rather as qualitative.

What remains is not a temporal but a qualitative fulfilment. The present is really intended to be different. Israel has not yet really taken hold of it; Israel has 'not as yet come to [its] rest'.[7]

In the admonition not to fall into idolatry, it is evident where Deuteronomy locates the failure. So now Deuteronomy impressively embodies, as it takes Israel back to the stage before the entry into the land, a second challenge to Israel to take its history seriously. The sphere in which time is now opened up for Israel is not, however, the sphere of a future that approaches in linear fashion. Time is here constituted in a different manner. Here time is not a temporal dimension, but rather a matter of environment.

To express the futuristic character of this difference, Deuteronomy places the people theologically once again at the beginning of the possession of the land. Through such a fictitious temporal future the existential future is to be made clear.[8]

Schmid undoubtedly refers to a significant state of affairs and one worthy of consideration. That which Deuteronomy represents to the contemporaries of Moses as yet future and as a promised gift that is almost within their grasp is, for those who live under the monarchy and are addressed in the Deuteronomic instruction, already fulfilled reality, particularly with respect to content, that is, the gift of the land. He is right in saying that beyond this Deuteronomy allows for no further historical step on the part of Yahweh in relation to his people, and in this sense therefore proposes no further futurist eschatology in the sense of a new kind of historical content beyond the gift of the land.

But does this correct statement of the case really justify as a conclusion: 'the present is the culmination of salvation history'? The situation in Deuteronomy is not substantially different from that in the priestly writings. There history moves toward the constitution of Israel as the people of God with its worship appointed by God, the worship appointed for the tent of meeting in the wilderness. We have indicated that in relation to this concern even the fulfilment of the promise of the land took second place. Thus it appears that according to the priestly writings God's act in salvation history had already reached fulfilment with Mount Sinai. One would then be required with Schmid to endorse the conclusion of the priestly writer, that the culmination of salvation-history had been already reached. The assertion of a qualitative prior element is just as appropriately applied to a salvation that is here already in the past. Then Israel would have to act in response not only to the present, as in Deuteronomy, but also to the past that already lies far behind it. We must repeat then about Deuteronomy what we have said about the priestly writings. Here as

there Israel had not, as Schmid formulates it, 'to maintain a relationship to its present' (or in that case its past), but rather a relationship to its God who remains the one who promises and effects
every event of salvation history, the one who is therefore the Lord
of all who is prior to and above history – the 'first and the last',
Second Isaiah will say. To be sure, it is very clear in Deuteronomy
that for Israel the saving gift of the land is the place where the
gracious approach of God is known. That beautiful prayer of
Deut. 26.5–11, in which the farmer, having harvested his gift,
appears before God with it, confessing that God has graciously
led first the fathers and then the nation and rendering his thanks in
the day of fulfilment, suffices to illustrate this. But it is not this
gift, not his acre of land to which the farmer must now relate himself, no matter how much even this land may be a sacramental
pledge of the gracious guidance of God; he must relate to the
commandment given to him by his God and therefore to God
himself. '. . . You shall love Yahweh your God with all your
heart, and with all your soul, and with all your might.' In this
sentence in the introductory section (6.5) all the commandments
are summarized.

By this call, however, which in all its commands places Israel
directly before God himself, Israel is summoned to decide whether
it will choose blessing or curse, behind which lie life and death and
so a future or else loss of future.

At the conclusion of the expansion in Deut. 29–30, in which the
giving of the law by Moses in Deuteronomy is seen as a special
covenant-making in the land of Moab, we hear (30.15f.):

See, I have set before you this day life and good, death and evil. If you
obey the commandments of Yahweh your God which I command you
this day, by loving Yahweh your God, by walking in his ways, and by
keeping his commandments and his statutes and his ordinances, then
you shall live and multiply, and Yahweh your God will bless you in the
land which you are entering to take possession of it. But if your heart
turns away. . . . I declare to you this day, that you shall perish; you
shall not live long in the land. . . . I have set before you life and death,
blessing and curse; therefore choose life, that you and your descendants
may live.

The fact that this is not just a call to an existential future is best
illustrated by a reference to ch. 28. Here at the conclusion of the
Deuteronomic law-giving, we see blessing and curse for the

obedience and disobedience of Israel, and it is clear how through this blessing and cursing a new history can unfold. Granted that no new events in the history of Israel are announced here in any striking way. But the possibility is demonstrated not only of blessing for nature but also of Israel's position in the world.

And the Lord will make you the head and not the tail; and you shall tend upward only, and not downward; if you obey the commandments of Yahweh your God, which I command you this day.. . . (v. 13)

But in these words lies the possibility of future history. A generation which stands before the mystery of the collapse of the northern kingdom, undoubtedly has very precise expectations. These are very clearly evident in the words of Jer. 3.6–13, which arise 'out of the days of Josiah'.

But above all our attention must now be focused on the Deuteronomistic historical work. This presents the history of the years following the entrance of Israel into the land from a somewhat later viewpoint after the catastrophe of 587 as illuminated by the Deuteronomic writers. It will make clear how Deuteronomic thought, although it appears to have arrived at the culmination of salvation-history, is able to grasp the troubled story from the time of Moses onwards, confessing it to be God's history in relation to his people.

In his *Überlieferungsgeschichtlichen Studien* of 1943, Noth has worked out the evidence for the fact that the narratives following Deuteronomy, the books of Joshua, Judges, Samuel and Kings, constitute a single coherently shaped work. Certainly an abundance of material already shaped and ready to hand is taken up and for the most part built into the narrative without the introduction of any alteration. It can clearly be seen that the combination of these materials makes for a complete story with very special perspectives if we look at two elements which exemplify an effect characteristic of the Deuteronomist: at important points he makes the leading actors step forward with a speech in which they look back and interpret the history of past experience and then look forward to draw practical conclusions for Israel's conduct. Thus in Josh. 1 and 23 we find speeches by Joshua, at the beginning and end of the conquest of the land. In I Sam. 12 a speech by Samuel marks off the end of the period of the judges and the beginning of that of the monarchy. Then there comes in I Kings

8.14ff. the great prayer of Solomon at the dedication of the temple in which the meaning of the temple is brought to light. The second feature of the Deuteronomist's composition is seen in the historical summaries: in Josh. 12 at the end of the conquest of the land, in Judg. 2.11ff. at the beginning of the period of the judges, and in II Kings 17.7ff. at the collapse of the northern kingdom of Israel. In what follows we shall seek to describe the view of history discernible in these sections and enquire what these implications were for the over-all theme of hope throughout the Deuteronomist's work.

Noth finds the beginning of the Deuteronomistic history in the speech of Moses in Deut. 1–3, which describes the experiences of the time of wilderness wanderings after the departure from Mount Sinai. This is followed by Deuteronomy's great exhortation to keep the commandments. Even those who differ from Noth, and think that the work does not begin until the book of Joshua, cannot overlook the clear reference back to the word of Deuteronomy in Joshua's opening speech in which he calls upon the people to move into the land.

Remember the word which Moses the servant of the Lord commanded you, saying 'Yahweh your God is providing you a place of rest, and will give you this land.' (Josh.1.13)

The same word is heard in the concluding speech of Joshua, whose work of conquest is summarized in a general survey in Josh. 12, a speech dated to the time 'when the Lord had given rest to Israel from all their enemies round about. . . .' (Josh. 23.1). In this speech Joshua declares, as he reflects on the great event of the possession of the land:

And now I am about to go the way of all the earth, and you know in your hearts and souls, all of you, that not one thing has failed of all the good things which Yahweh your God promised concerning you; all have come to pass for you, not one of them has failed. (Josh. 23.14)

Ought we not to speak here of a culminating point of salvation history? The broader context, however, makes clear that the intention here is not by any means to speak of the end of the history of God's dealings with his people. As the speech continues it is emphasized that nothing has been withdrawn of the stern word of threat that God has spoken to those who will not obey the covenant he has appointed (23.15f.).

This admonitory tone also dominates the preceding words that refer back expressly to the law of Moses:

Therefore be very steadfast to keep and do all that is written in the book of the law of Moses, turning aside from it neither to the right hand nor to the left. (23.6)

Here the darker tones are clearly audible, insisting that the history of God's dealings with his people can also become a story of wrath and of the loss of the land. This dark tone governs even more clearly the curious historical reflection of the time of the judges in Judg. 2.11ff., which introduces the stories of the individual judges. Again and again during this period we hear this verdict:

They forsook Yahweh, the God of their fathers, who had brought them out of the land of Egypt; they went after other gods, from among the gods of the peoples who were round about them, and bowed to them. ... (Judg. 2.12)

And then Yahweh's anger is kindled against them, and he gives them over into the hands of their enemies. But when they cry out again to Yahweh, he has compassion in response to their wailing and sends them a saviour in the person of a judge. The farewell speech of Samuel, the last judge, in I Sam. 12, which stands at the end of the strangely troubled time of the judges, and is marked by the same negative stress on the disobedience of Israel upon whom the preserving hand of Yahweh then once again becomes visible, introduces a new historical period. The people have wished for a king, such as all the neighbouring peoples have. Then Yahweh, according to I Sam. 8.7, comforts the perplexed Samuel with the dismal consolation, 'They have not rejected you, but they have rejected me from being king over them', and then commands him to grant the wish of the people. In his farewell address Samuel admonishes the people, who are belatedly shaken by his action:

Fear not; you have done all this evil, yet do not turn aside from following Yahweh, but serve Yahweh with all your heart. (I Sam. 12.20)

This is the question which, according to the Deuteronomist, the people must face during the period of the kings: Will the people be able to remain obedient under the special dangers which the monarchy stands for? The Deuteronomist takes up a further rich vein of historical traditions about the first three kings, Saul, David, and Solomon, traditions which are to a large extent incorporated unchanged into his narrative. This material includes the report of the promise which in II Sam. 7 the prophet Nathan speaks of David and his house, and which, as will become clear, is not without significance for the Deuteronomist's own view of the period of the monarchy. A far-reaching promise breaks anew into the history of God's dealings with his people. It is a new kind of promise in which God now pledges to David that he will build him a house, that is, give him a future and descendants. But simultaneously there is already in this chapter in v. 13a – a Deuteronomistic elaboration – a preliminary reference to the construction of the temple of Solomon.

As is clear from the insertion of Solomon's extended prayer at the dedication of the temple in I Kings 8.15–53 and from the blessing in 8.56–61, this creates an important new element in the history of Israel as related by the writer. Again we hear the echo of words from the beginning, as the blessing opens with the words:

Blessed be Yahweh who has given rest to his people Israel, according to all that he promised; not one word has failed of all his good promise, which he uttered by Moses his servant. (I Kings 8.56)

The words of praise in the light of the promise fulfilled, which are spoken in the book of Joshua at the time of the occupation of the land, are here spoken anew on the occasion of the dedication of the temple. By this the Deuteronomist obviously means to convey that the history of God's dealings moves toward the fulfilment of the more recent promises. In this prayer at the dedication of the temple it is also striking that any reference to sacrificial worship is completely absent. The temple is understood in good Deuteronomic fashion as the dwelling place of the name of Yahweh. It is by his *name* that Yahweh is called upon. Thus the earnest prayer is offered that Yahweh may hear the appeal that takes place here. Yes, the case is even considered in which the people might be led away into a far country: if they repent there, so Solomon begs, and direct their prayers from far off toward this place, then may God hear them (vv. 46ff.). Here there is already an unmistakable allusion to the period after 587. Nor is the tone of sorrow over the possible disobedience of the people absent from this prayer. In the closing blessing we hear:

Yahweh our God be with us . . . that he may incline our hearts to him, to walk in all his ways, and to keep his commandments, his statutes, and his ordinances, which he commanded our fathers. (vv. 57f.)

What Solomon here prays is turned against Solomon himself by Yahweh in the account of God's second appearance to him in I Kings 9.1ff. Alongside the blessing which is promised to obedience, there emerges here fully elaborated a threat that disobedience will lead to the extermination of Israel from the land and the destruction of the temple, so that the passers-by will conclude:

Because they forsook Yahweh their God who brought their fathers out of the land of Egypt, and laid hold on other gods, and worshipped them and served them; therefore Yahweh has brought all this evil upon them. (I Kings 9.9)

This dark possibility of unfaithfulness begins even as early as the time of Solomon to characterize the history of Israel.

After the division of the kingdom under Solomon's son, the northern kingdom is the first to pave the way for its own downfall with the worship of the images of the golden calf set up at Bethel and Dan. In the characteristic form of the Deuteronomistic account of the kings, which deals out a censure to each king, all the kings of the northern kingdom are pronounced to be sinners, so that the fall of the northern kingdom is destined of inner necessity. II Kings 17.7f. provides, with the last insertion of a more general Deuteronomistic comment, the foundation for this judgment: the sin of Israel, its worship of other gods, the worship on high places, pillars and Asherim, and, in all this, the unwillingness to listen to the warnings of the prophets, whom God untiringly sent to warn them – all these are the reasons for its downfall.

The elaboration in vv. 19f. then extends this judgment just as fully to Judah:

Judah also did not keep the commandments of Yahweh their God. . . . And Yahweh rejected all the descendants of Israel, and afflicted them, and gave them into the hand of spoilers, until he had cast them out of his sight.

Thus the history of the kings of Judah, who are measured above all else by the criterion of worship in high places outside Jerusalem, shows that the very few devout ones, a Hezekiah and a Josiah, are not able to counterbalance the excessive godlessness of the others, above all a Manasseh. Judah also ends up in exile. Jerusalem and its temple go up in flames.

What is this whole Deuteronomistic history, which we have been able to sketch above only in outline, seeking to tell us? Has it also something to say about hope and a future for mankind? Noth answers this question with a blunt no. The narrator who speaks in this work stands at an end.

He has seen, in the divine judgment consummated in the outward collapse of the people of Israel as he presents it, something that is apparently final and conclusive and that does not once give expression to a future hope even in the humblest and simplest form of an expectation of a future gathering of the dispersed exiles.[9]

The answer that G. von Rad gives is fundamentally different.[10] He shows on the one hand how the word of prophetic prediction, which is then as a rule followed by the report of its fulfilment, runs through the entire historical recital of the books of Kings and gives it a characteristic disposition toward redemption. In the ultimate destiny vindication finally triumphs. Here can be recognized the discharge of the curse which is already envisaged as a possibility in Moses' preaching of the law in Deuteronomy. Alongside this von Rad emphasizes the final episode of II Kings, according to which King Jehoiachin, after thirty-seven years of imprisonment in Babylon, is freed on the ascension to the throne of King Evil-merodach, and is set on high at the table of the king of Babylon. It is in this connection that we should evaluate the repeated references in the narrative of Kings to Yahweh 'for David's sake' bestowing special grace on his individual successors. Alongside the law that runs through the history of Israel, judging and destroying, is seen here, on the basis of the promise given to David (II Sam. 7), a gospel at work, saving and forgiving.

It is the promise to Nathan that runs through the history of Judah like a κατέχων and wards off the long merited judgment from the kingdom for the sake of David.[11]

It is in this light that he believes one can understand that remarkable final episode as an expression of hope 'that the line of David has not yet come to an irrevocable end'.[12]

In his study of the Deuteronomistic history H. W. Wolff[13] believes that he also must reject this point of view. According to him the Deuteronomistic narrator sees no future which he has to proclaim. His whole narrative, as the repeated appearance of statements on the subject demonstrates, is intended as a call to repentance. But Wolff[14] has himself demonstrated at other points that the call to repentance in the Old Testament has nowhere simply the character of an absolute demand, but rather is always given against the background of a consciousness of the approach of God.

Wolff is correct, to be sure, when he rejects any suggestion of hearing an open and public promise in the Deuteronomist's account. But must it not in any case be said that throughout his entire story, which speaks of the righteous judgment of God upon his sinful people, he recognizes the living God at work, the one who according to II Sam. 7 uttered concerning David his promise of a future for David's sons and who, according to I Kings 8, pledges to hear his people in the place which he has chosen for his name to dwell? None of this is presented by the Deuteronomist with the accent of absolute certainty. But throughout his entire narrative, in which he recounts so often, beginning with the days of the judges, the amazing approach of Yahweh to the cry of need by his people, we hear this 'perhaps' which was heard even in Lam. 3.29, even in the days after the destruction of Jerusalem. 'Let him put his mouth in the dust – there may yet be hope.' But there it was evident that this 'perhaps' arose from the inner certainty:

The steadfast love of Yahweh never ceases, his mercies never come to an end; they are new every morning; great is thy faithfulness. 'Yahweh is my portion,' says my soul, 'therefore I will hope in him.' (3.22-24)

NOTES

[1] M. Noth, *Überlieferungsgeschichtliche Studien I. Die sammelnden und bearbeitenden Geschichtswerke im Alten Testament* (Schriften der Königsberger Gelehrten Gesellschaft, 18. Jahr. Geisteswissenschaftliche Klasse, Heft 2, Halle/Saale 1943).
[2] A. Alt, 'Die Heimat des Deuteronomiums', *KlSchr* II, pp. 250-75.
[3] See e.g. the comparison in G. von Rad, *Deuteronomy* (OTL, 1966), p. 13.
[4] H. H. Schmid, 'Das Verständnis der Geschichte im Deuteronomium', *ZTK* 64 (1967), pp. 1-15.
[5] *Op. cit.*, p. 9.
[6] *Ibid.*, p. 10.

7 *Ibid.*, p. 11.
8 *Ibid.*, p. 13.
9 *Überlieferungsgeschichtliche Studien*, p. 108.
10 G. von Rad, *Studies in Deuteronomy* (SBT 9, 1953).
11 *Ibid.*, p. 89.
12 *Ibid.*, p. 91.
13 H. W. Wolff, 'Das Kerygma des deuteronomistischen Geschichtswerks', *ZAW* 73 (1961), pp. 171–86 (= *Gesammelte Studien zum Alten Testament*, ThB 22, 1964, pp. 308–24).
14 H. W. Wolff, 'Das Thema "Umkehr" in der alttestamentlichen Prophetie', *ZTK* 48 (1951), pp. 129–48 (= *Gesammelte Studien zum Alten Testament*, pp. 130–50).

VII

THE PROPHETIC WRITINGS OF THE
EIGHTH CENTURY

ACCORDING to the Deuteronomistic history we have just been
considering, prophets repeatedly took a prominent part in the
history of the Kings of Israel. In their proclamation of the word of
Yahweh they had the task of opening up the present to what
was coming. They were to announce the act of God that would
subsequently take on the character of a word fulfilled. These
Deuteronomistic accounts mediate only a weak impression of what
actually happened with the appearance of the great prophets,
whom we know more clearly from the written collections of their
words and whom we therefore normally designate as the writing
prophets. The next two chapters will be given over to a description
of the future expectations and hopes of Israel as they are reflected
in the words of these prophets.

The great prophetic writings are contemporary with the stormy
phase of Near Eastern history from the eighth to the sixth century
before the Christian era.[1] During this period the Assyrians made a
clean sweep of the little states in the area between the Tigris-
Euphrates valley and Egypt. They in their turn were overrun by
the Neo-Babylonians and the Medes in the second half of the
seventh century. Then after the middle of the sixth century there
arose in the realm of the Medes, breaking their dominance and that
of the Lydians, and finally also of the Neo-Babylonians, the power
of Persia, which then near the end of the century also annexed
Egypt, until then only from time to time subdued by the
Assyrians. Israel, living at the beginning of this period as two
separate political units, was to be wiped out politically during this
period. The greater and politically more important northern
kingdom, that more particularly bore the name of Israel, was laid
low as early as 722, as we mentioned above, by the onslaught of the

Assyrians. The smaller state of Judah with Jerusalem, the seat of power for the House of David, held out scarcely one hundred and fifty years longer. Then in 587 it also succumbed to the Neo-Babylonians under their King Nebuchadnezzar II (605–562). At the beginning of the Persian period it became possible under Persian sovereignty and as a part of the province of Samaria to create in and around Jerusalem a small state of an ecclesiastical type with its centre in a second Jerusalem temple.

The message of the writing prophets cannot be understood apart from this series of events. This is true not only in the general sense in which this like any other historical phenomenon cannot be understood without knowledge of the historical background from which it lives. This holds in the much deeper sense in which this event is a part of their message. In this event their word becomes history – a word that, without its character as event demonstrated by history, would remain empty human opinion and therefore not a prophetic word, a word from God.

It is expressive of the character of the prophetic word, bound as it is to the political events in Israel, that it is first heard in that part of Israel in its wider sense in which the political centre of gravity of all Israel lies – in the northern kingdom, in 'Israel' in its narrower sense. Alongside the prophet whose homeland is there, Hosea, there stands also the prophet who came to the northern kingdom from Judah, Amos. This second-named prophet in fact preached somewhat earlier than Hosea, who belonged to the northern kingdom. Suddenly and with little preparation that we can see, the prophetic word breaks forth in the proclamation of Amos.[2] This proclamation, the first written collection of the words of a prophet, is recorded only because as a consequence of his preaching he is forbidden to speak in Israel with the cheap excuse that he is a foreigner. The written word keeps his witness alive and leaves Israel without excuse when destruction comes. Let no one say then that God did not make his word heard in good time. Amos is a storm signal in the midst of an externally calm, even prospering and progressive period of Israel's history. Under King Jeroboam II Israel had successfully resisted in a way hopeful for the future its traditional deadly enemy, Aram-Damascus, with whom it had frequently engaged in battle during the past hundred years and under whom it had suffered terribly. It had thus achieved victory on its north-east border. Who would have suspected then that crippling the Arameans from Damascus would open the door for the arrival of a still harsher and greater power from the East, whose pressure Damascus already felt. Thus the words of Amos allow us an insight into the hope of the people – not a godless superficial hope, but hope for a further bright future from the hand of the God who had chosen Israel and led it out of Egypt. This hope is directed especially towards the coming 'Day of Yahweh' – that is, a future in which Yahweh would draw near to his people with new help. When we seek a more precise understanding of the hope for the 'Day of Yahweh', opinions are contradictory. Gressmann[3] thinks that we encounter in this expression the expectation of an eschatological crisis based ultimately on a mythical view of the world. But von Rad[4] attempts to understand this hope more directly from Israel's historical past, with its experience of Yahweh's intervention on behalf of his people in holy wars. The question need not be answered here. It is enough if we see in this expectation of the 'Day of Yahweh' a hope of Israel that does not ignore Yahweh, but is directed wholly toward him and sees in his coming the foundation for a bright future.

What does Amos have to say about this hope of Israel, which has surely been formulated correctly according to all our investigations up to this point. His word can terrify:

> Woe unto you who desire [hope for] the day of Yahweh!
>   Why would you have the day of Yahweh?
> It is darkness and not light;
>   as if a man fled from a lion,
>   and a bear met him,
> or went into the house and leaned with his hand against the wall,
>   and a serpent bit him.
> Is not the day of Yahweh darkness and not light,
>   and gloom with no brightness in it? (Amos 5.18–20)

Yes, says Amos, you have a future and this future is God himself. And precisely because this is so, you have nothing to hope for. Does Amos then know nothing of that original approach of God to his people, in which he had turned to his people in mercy. Certainly he is aware of this:

Hear this word that Yahweh has spoken against you, O people of Israel, against the whole family which I brought up out of the land of Egypt:

> 'You only have I known
> of all the families of the earth;
> therefore I will punish you
> for all your iniquities.' (3.1f.)

But as his hearers take up the assertion that God has led his people out of Egypt, he can respond with uncomfortably cutting words:

> 'Are you not like the Ethiopians to me,
> O people of Israel?' says Yahweh.
> 'Did I not bring up Israel from the land of Egypt,
> and the Philistine from Caphtor and the Syrians from Kir?' (9.7)

What has become of the special hope of Israel?

Only in one word, which at the same time reveals why Israel is addressed with this stern and merciless message, does there appear peripherally some possibility of hope and of a future. In the style of priestly instruction in the law, Amos says:

> Seek good, and not evil,
> that you may live;
> and so the Lord, the God of hosts, will be with you,
> as you have said.
> Hate evil, and love good,
> and establish justice in the gate;
> it may be that Yahweh, the God of hosts,
> will be gracious to the remnant of Joseph. (5.14f.)[5]

The blind unconcerned neglect of the law of God in Israel makes Amos certain that this people has no hope, but rather that their encounter with their God will mean their end. Thus one of the visions of Amos issues in the gloomy proclamation: 'The end has come upon my people Israel; I will never again pass by them [spare them]' (8.2). Only if it should come to pass that God's people learned to love the law of God, a law especially concerned for the poor, from their heart, would it be possible to hope for divine mercy toward the remnant of Joseph. 'Perhaps'–in this word lies a reference to the freedom of God, which not even the most devout behaviour of men can limit. This was the point on which Job had insisted against his friends. 'The remnant of Joseph' – in this there lies the certainty that there is no longer any way round the judgment of God for Israel in the days of Amos. Only for the remnant preserved through this judgment is it possible for this 'perhaps' to mean a future and a hope.

In the last verses of the book of Amos this future appears to take on more definite lines. 9.11f. speaks of the restoration of the ruins of the Booth of David as it once was, and vv. 13–15 describe the unusual productivity of the land in the time when Yahweh again restores the fortunes of his people and enables them to rebuild their cities. But there is a strong suspicion that here a happier conclusion may have been added later to Amos's message of disaster. This is given support by the fact that in the second passage a deportation and devastation of the land appears to be presupposed. Thus it is necessary to consider seriously the possibility that in his preaching Amos does not go beyond that 'perhaps'.

Israel's euphoria in the days of Amos does not last for long. Hosea,[6] speaking somewhat later, gives us considerable insight into the unrest in Israel after the death of Jeroboam. In the midst of the political infighting and confusion over the succession described in detail in II Kings, there stands out ever more clearly the shadow of the great power to the east which under the mighty warrior-king Tiglath Pileser III (745–727) begins to take a share in the shaping of history. But Hosea also speaks, as did Amos, however different his human style, not of any particular danger to Israel from external powers, but of Yahweh as Israel's most dangerous enemy.

In fierce savage images the Lord, who should be Israel's own special hope, presses upon his people in the prophetic word:

> For I will be like a lion to Ephraim,
>   and like a young lion to the house of Judah.
> I, even I, will rend and go away,
>   I will carry off, and none shall rescue. (Hos. 5.14)

According to the analysis of A. Alt[7] this word should be dated at the time of the so called Syrian-Ephraimite war, an event which also lies behind the words of Isaiah 7. Judah and Israel stand together in this struggle. But behind both stands the Assyrian power as a great danger but also, because of its tremendous potential as a helper, a much-wooed giant. If we ask why Yahweh appears in such sinister guise in the words of Hosea just quoted as the destroyer of all hope for the two Israelite states, then the words directly preceding make clear that by no means the least reason for this is that both these states have directed their hopes and expectations to this earthly power:

> When Ephraim saw his sickness,
>   and Judah his wound,
> then Ephraim went to Assyria,
>   and sent to the great king.
> But he is not able to cure you
>   or heal your wound. (Hos. 5.13)

It would be incorrect to assume that in the days of Hosea the people whom God was addressing had simply forgotten him. In 6.1–3, as part of the words of the prophet, a song of lamentation is quoted in which the people turn to Yahweh even in the midst of their present political distress and sickness.

Come, let us return to Yahweh; for he has torn, that he may heal us; he has stricken, and he will bind us up.

> After two days he will revive us;
>   on the third day he will raise us up,
>   that we may live before him.
> Let us know, let us press on to know Yahweh;
>   his going forth is sure as the dawn;
> he will come to us as the showers,
>   as the spring rains that water the earth.

With these words Israel's hope in God as the one who is able to give life is given impressive formulation. It is reminiscent in its wording of those audacious marginal notes in Ps. 73 and Job 19 in which hope drives through death and beyond toward the possibility of the divine gift of life.

There is much to suggest that the words of prayer depend on formulations having their origin in the realm of Canaanite fertility gods. We may also feel certain that in this song a contrite willingness to return to Yahweh is expressed. And yet Yahweh rejects this return and this hope in his life-giving power:

> What shall I do with you, O Ephraim?
> What shall I do with you, O Judah?
> Your love is like a morning cloud,
>   like the dew that goes early away. (6.4)

This prayer, apparently accompanied with lavish sacrificial offerings, does not arise out of a truly faithful dependence on God, does not demonstrate the love faithful to the covenant which God looks for:

> For I desire steadfast love and not sacrifice,
>   the knowledge of God, rather than burnt offerings. (6.6)

Because God cannot see in his people, even as they approach him with an abundance of sacrificial offerings, the determination of authentic faithfulness and the clear recognition, bound up with fitting acknowledgement in their lives, that he alone is Israel's hope, his stern rejection stands. This is formulated with conceivably even greater severity in the horrifying symbolic acts with which the prophet at the outset is assigned his prophetic ministry. He must marry a harlot, 'for the land commits great harlotry by forsaking Yahweh' (1.2). He must give his second child, a daughter, the name *lo ruḥāmā*, 'Not pitied', 'for I will no more have pity on the house of Israel' (1.6). His third child, a son, receives the name *lo ʿammī*, 'Not My People', 'for you are not my people and I am not your God'[8] (1.9).

But then we see that alongside this in Hosea something else emerges with apparently incomprehensible lack of logic. Not the 'perhaps' of Amos, which came to be possible on the basis of the better righteousness of a remnant people. It is evident in 11.8f. that his something else can emerge directly from the heart of God himself. Here a stern speech of judgment against the people, once a son called out of Egypt by Yahweh but then insolently despising his love, breaks off with the words:

> How can I give you up, O Ephraim!
>   How can I hand you over, O Israel! . . .
> My heart recoils within me,
>   my compassion grows warm and tender.
> I will not execute my fierce anger,
>   I will not again destroy Ephraim;
> for I am God and not man,
>   the Holy One in your midst. . . .

And therefore Hosea 3 reports for the second time a symbolic act in which Hosea lawfully acquires an adulterous woman, and subjects her to severe disciplinary confinement:

'You must dwell as mine for many days; you shall not play the harlot, or belong to another man; so will I also be to you.' For the children of Israel shall dwell many days without king or prince, without sacrifice or pillar, without ephod or teraphim. Afterward the children of Israel shall return and seek the Lord their God. . . . (3.3–5)

When David is mentioned here as their king, this may be seen as a Judaic expansion of the text. This connects the expectation here with lines of thought which can be discovered in Isaiah.

Chapter 11 makes it clear that for the northern Israelite, Hosea, it is the Exodus from Egypt that represents historically the initial act of the love of Yahweh. It is against this background that we are to understand 12.9 as it says in the context of a threat: 'I am the Lord your God from the land of Egypt; I will again make you dwell in tents, as in the days of the appointed feast.' And this mysterious mingling of anger, judgment, and mercy can be seen even more readily in 2.14f., where Yahweh says:

> Therefore, behold, I will allure her,
>   and bring her into the wilderness,
>   and speak tenderly to her.
> And there I will give her her vineyards,
>   and make the Valley of Achor a door of hope.
> And there she shall answer as in the days of her youth,
>   as at the time when she came out of the land of Egypt.

The wealth of the land of Canaan with all its productivity will be taken away from Israel. It will again know poverty and dwell in tents away out in the wilderness, will experience a period of strict seclusion. But even in this poverty God will again speak tenderly to it and the people will again be able to become his people. And then when Yahweh once more leads his people into the land, through the valley of Achor where according to Josh. 7.26 a heap of stones is a reminder of the stoning of Achan who at the first entry into the land had brought trouble to the people by his sin, this valley will become a door of hope. The key-word 'hope' (*tiqwāh*) has expressly to do with the event that Israel faces and which 2.20f. perfectly describes as a new betrothal of Yahweh to his people. This is the future which Israel, whose present is identified with the picture of a prostitute and an adulteress, may approach through judgment and poverty as a great hope.

The northern kingdom was destroyed shortly after days in which Hosea preached. It is not beyond the bounds of possibility that Hosea himself was a witness of this judgment. All that remained was the little remnant of Judah which, however, sheltered the temple of Solomon and the king of the tribe of David. But we can see that here in the south also the prophetic word is heard.

And here also we find two very different figures. Alongside the city dweller, Isaiah, who lived in the vicinity of the court of the house of David and in whose words old Jerusalem traditions are heard, there is Micah, the man from Moreseth Gath, a place in the Judean countryside which lay near the Philistine border. Both, however, are awestruck as they perceive the approaching step of the God of Israel in the history of their days. And from this insight the eyes of both are opened to the general disregard of divine justice and the resulting collapse of any just social order in which even the least receive their share.

In detail, however, their proclamation takes on very different accents. For Micah,[9] the man from the country, the sins of the people are concentrated essentially in the major cities: 'What is the transgression of Jacob? Is it not Samaria? And what is the sin of the house of Judah? Is it not Jerusalem?' (Micah 1.5). So then he sees these centres of offence especially threatened by the judgment-stroke of God. In a word that must have struck home unusually hard – one hundred years later the elders of the land still talked of it in connection with the judicial proceedings against Jeremiah (Jer. 26.18) – he announces with great severity the complete devastation not only of the city of Jerusalem but also of the temple, the place of the holy dwelling of God: 'Therefore because of you, Zion shall be ploughed as a field; Jerusalem shall become a heap of ruins, and the mountain of the house a wooded height' (Micah 3.12).

Does Micah have any conception of hope for his land beyond all this catastrophe? Among the words that we can attribute to him with any certainty, this appears to be the case only in 5.2–6, a word that has undergone a thorough reworking at a later time. Out of a setting, whose beginning is familiar from the Christmas story in Matthew (2.6), the following sentences may belong to Micah:

> But you, O Bethlehem Ephrathah [or originally: Beth Ephrath?],
>   who are little to be among the clans of Judah,
> from you shall come forth for me
>   one who is to be ruler in Israel,
> whose origin is from of old,
>   from ancient days . . .
> And he shall stand and feed his flock in the strength of Yahweh,
>   in the majesty of the name of Yahweh his God . . .

> And this shall be peace, . . .
> and he shall deliver us from the Assyrian
>   when he comes into our land
>   and treads within our border.

It is noteworthy that here also the hopeful future which Micah announces in the midst of his otherwise stern proclamation calls the people back again to the beginning of their history. As once from the politically insignificant clan of Ephrath, of Bethlehem, God had raised up a saviour from the oppression of the Philistines, so in the time of trouble when the Assyrian threat to make an end of Jerusalem hangs over it, a ruler will be called from that ancient clan to turn aside the Assyrian blow. Perhaps we may associate with this the word which A. Alt[10] hears in Micah 2.1-5. After the great catastrophe which robs the landowners of their land, there will be in Jerusalem a new and more just division of the land in which there will be no more unjust acquisition of land by anyone. 'Therefore you will have none to cast the line over the portion of land in the assembly of Yahweh' (2.5). These words are not spiritual in meaning, but deal with concrete political realities: the new ruler, a deliverer from the oppression of rule by others, creates a new system of property ownership. But the unusual feature in all this is that the new ruler, like David, comes from the rural clan of Ephrath. Perhaps it is even the same old family in mind here. He will have nothing to do with the Davidic kingdom established in Jerusalem at that time. In this expectation also there exists a hope in Yahweh. If a king is to be expected who will be a warrior in the struggle against Assyria, he will do what he does in the strength and name of Yahweh. He is the one who once again calls his ruler from the improbable little place and so demonstrates again that what seems insignificant to man can receive strength and honour from him. This is Micah's proclamation of the future toward which he calls his people to hope.

How entirely different is the word of Isaiah.[11] The account of his call, related by Isaiah himself in ch. 6, leads us into the Temple in Jerusalem. Here the burning closeness of his God, whom in the terminology of the royal sanctuary he identifies as a king, Yahweh Sabaoth, Yahweh of Hosts, overwhelms him. Here, after he has been absolved of his guilt and prepared to be a messenger in response to his offer, he receives the difficult assignment of driving the people to impenitence. 'Until cities lie waste without inhabitant, and houses without men, and the land is utterly desolate' he is to carry out his hard task (6.11). It is a matter of debate as to whether the short concluding remark about the stump of a felled tree, which sheds a ray of hope over the stern commission with the words 'the holy seed is its stump', belongs to the original text.

It is further important to observe the way in which this prophet accompanies the shifting events of the second half of the eighth century with his proclamation. Called in the year of the death of King Uzziah at a still relatively peaceful time, he is witness to the invasion of the Assyrians under Tiglath Pileser III into Syrian territory and the impending collapse of northern Israel. In the so-called Syrian-Ephraimite war Damascus and north Israel attempt to create a defensive alliance in Syria-Palestine and to force Judah under King Ahaz into this alliance.

This provokes new attacks by the Assyrians who crush Damascus and reduce Israel to a quarter of its former extent. Isaiah experiences the further convulsions of resistance in Palestine which bring the northern kingdom to an end, reduce the Philistine states of the coastlands to greater subjection, and bring Judah to the verge of complete destruction. During the time of the Syrian-Ephraimite war, Judah had given itself into the protection and so also the domination of Assyria and had then attempted to loosen its chains. The words of Isaiah in 1.4–9, which are perhaps his last, make clear how Sennacherib laid waste the countryside of Judah in the year 701 and left King Hezekiah with only his capital as the tiny remnant of his kingdom after the capitulation of Jerusalem.

> If Yahweh of hosts
>   had not left us a few survivors,
> we should have been like Sodom,
>   and become like Gomorrah.
>
> The whole head is sick,
>   and the whole heart faint.
> From the sole of the foot even to the head,
>   there is no soundness in it,
> but bruises and sores
>   and bleeding wounds;
> they are not pressed out, or bound up,
>   or softened with oil. (vv. 9,5b–6)

So run the complaints of the prophet, as he sees his people wounded and struck down on all sides.

This is the outcome of more than forty years of proclamation by the prophet. Is there any room left for hope and expectation by Israel? To be sure, the prophet knows of Yahweh's own expectation and hope, which are repeatedly disappointed by his people. In the 'song of the vineyard' in which he compares God's concern for his people with the concern of a vineyard owner for his vineyard, he says of this owner,

> He looked (*qwh*) for it to yield grapes
> but it yielded wild grapes. (5.2b)

Further on we hear the complaining question of the vineyard owner,

> What more was there to do for my vineyard,
> that I have not done in it?
> When I looked (*qwh*) for it to yield grapes,
> why did it yeild wild grapes? (5.4)

But even the prophet tears away all pictorial wrappings:

> For the vineyard of the Yahweh of hosts
> is the house of Israel,
> and the men of Judah
> are his pleasant planting;
> and he looked (*qwh*) for the good act,
> but behold the blood act,
> for emulation of the right,
> but behold violation of the right! (5.7)

The word-play jars the ears of the hearer, as the proposed translation of the original Hebrew text attempts to suggest. In view of this frequent disappointment of God's hope by the people, can there be a message of hope for man?

In the light of the situation it may be surprising to detect in the prophet's own attitude precisely at the time of his deepest disappointment something of such an expectation. Near the end of the collection of words from the Syrian-Ephraimite war in which Isaiah saw that Yahweh offered his people new possibilities for life only to have them rejected with their choice of King Ahaz, and in which he made his message known through the symbolic names given to his children, we hear this word of Isaiah:

Bind up the testimony, seal the teaching among my disciples. I will wait (hope – *ḥkh*) for the Lord, who is hiding his face from the house of Jacob, and I will hope (*qwh*) in him. Behold, I and the children whom the Lord has given me are signs and portents in Israel from the Lord of hosts, who dwells on Mount Zion. (8.16–18)

It is a waiting and not a despairing. Isaiah knows that God's dealings with his people are not yet at an end.

And this is, in fact, recognizable in the proclamation of the prophet. In all the change which through the different historical phases Isaiah experiences in quick succession and which gives his proclamation a fluidity as with no other prophet, there appears again and again the proclamation of a final turn of events in which Yahweh will achieve victory for his purposes.

Isaiah's days are shaped by the invasion of the great power from the east. In the Assyrian Isaiah recognizes God's instrument of punishment with which he renders judgment upon all the arrogance and violation of justice which he sees in the land. But then the prophet sees how this instrument behaves without restraint and with arrogance, and tramples God's justice underfoot. And so he directs his word against this instrument of God's justice as well:

> Ah, Assyria, the rod of my anger,
>   the staff of my fury!
> Against a godless nation I send him,
>   and against the people of my wrath I command him,
> to take spoil and seize plunder,
>   and to tread them down like the mire of the streets.
> But he does not so intend,
>   and his mind does not so think;
> but it is in his mind to destroy,
>   and to cut off nations not a few. (10.5–7)

The prophet knows that the judgment of Yahweh must fall on Assyria also:

When the Lord has finished all his work on Mount Zion and on Jerusalem he will punish the arrogant boasting of the King of Assyria and his haughty pride. (10.12)

14.24ff. formulates it in an oath of Yahweh:

As I have planned,
  so shall it be,
and as I have purposed,
  so shall it stand,
that I will break the Assyrian in my land,
  and upon my mountains trample him under foot;
and his yoke shall depart from them,
  and his burden from their shoulder.
This is the purpose that is purposed
  concerning the whole earth;
and this is the hand that is stretched out
  over all the nations.[12]

But in order that, in all this, Yahweh's threat of judgment against
his own people may not simply be forgotten, an emphatic word
against Jerusalem is voiced in 29.1ff. Jerusalem is addressed as the
city of Ariel, which may refer to the altar hearth on which the
sacrifice is burned, and so indicate that the following is clearly a
play on words:

Ho Ariel, Ariel,
  The city where David encamped . . .
I will distress Ariel,
  and there shall be moaning and lamentation,
  and she shall be to me like an Ariel [altar hearth].
And I will encamp against you round about,
  and will besiege you with towers
  and I will raise siegeworks against you.
Then deep from the earth you shall speak,
  from low in the dust your words shall come . . .
And in an instant, suddenly,
  you will be visited by the Lord of hosts
with thunder and with earthquake and great noise,
  with whirlwind and tempest, and the flame of a
    devouring fire.
And the multitude of all the nations that fight against
    Ariel,
  all that fight against her and her stronghold and
    distress her,
  shall be like a dream, a vision of the night.[13]

It has been pointed out with justification that there are present
here motifs connected with the salvation of Zion which can also
be recognized in several Zion psalms (46, 48, 76) and which possibly

derive from old Jerusalem traditions. But we should notice how
Isaiah talks about this salvation of Zion, this mysteriously 'strange'
or 'alien' work of God, as it is called in 28.21. In a word spoken in
the year in which King Ahaz died, at a time when Isaiah, confronted with the rejoicing of the Philistine cities under the dangerous delusion of the decline of the Assyrian, announces the sinister
approach of the Assyrians which will transform this rejoicing into
crying (14.28–32), he receives also the task of giving a mysterious
answer to messengers of Philistia who apparently come to induce
Judah to join them:

> The Lord has founded Zion,
> and in her the afflicted of his people find refuge.

Here is the word that Zion is a refuge for those who reject arrogance
and self-sufficiency before God. The same thing is said in other
words in 28.16:

> Behold I am laying in Zion for a foundation
> a stone, a tested stone,

[the word appears to have its counterpart in Egyptian and to indicate a
dark hard stone that is used for monuments, chapels, obelisks][14]

> a precious cornerstone, of a sure foundation:
> 'He who believes will not be in haste.'

Here again Zion is identified as the place where the new thing
which will stand against all danger will be established. Whoever
believes, whoever acknowledges his own poverty in dependence
on Yahweh, may know himself safe and secure there. It is therefore clear that the prophet does not simply call for a general hope
for the salvation of Zion but knows something of division of the
people and decision by the people. May we link to this the fact that
in another context he speaks about a remnant? In connection with
the exciting events at the beginning of the Syrian-Ephraimite war
as reported in chapter 7, he is called of God to go to King Ahaz
and take his son *šeᶜarjašūb* with him. This son is called 'a remnant
returns'. The prophetic ambiguity leaves it open whether we
should understand this to mean 'only a remnant returns from the
war', which would make this a threatening word about approaching catastrophe, or whether it should be translated 'a remnant will
return', i.e., to Yahweh, and so experience salvation. For this is
the impression given in 30.15:

> In returning and rest you shall be saved;
>> in quietness and in trust shall be your strength.

But at the same time the prophet must say:

> And you would not, but you said,
> 'No! We will speed upon horses,'
>> therefore you shall speed away;
> and 'We will ride upon swift steeds,'
>> therefore your pursuers shall be swift.

Hope for salvation and present agony over the people of God are strikingly linked in the 'song of lamentation' ingeniously constructed in two sections in 1.21–26:

> How the faithful city
>> has become a harlot,
>> she that was full of justice!
> Righteousness lodged in her,
>> but now murderers.
> Your silver has become dross,
>> your wine mixed with water.
> Your princes are rebels
>> and companions of thieves.
> Everyone loves a bribe
>> and runs after gifts . . .
> Therefore the Lord says,
>> Yahweh of hosts,
>> the Mighty One of Israel:
> 'Ah, I will vent my wrath on my enemies,
>> and avenge myself on my foes.
> I will turn my hand against you
>> and will smelt away your dross as with lye
>> and remove all your alloy.
> And I will restore your judges as at the first,
>> and your counsellors as at the beginning.
> Afterward you shall be called the city of righteousness,
>> the faithful city.'

Here we have the heat of the fire into which the impure metal is thrown and through which all impurity is separated out. Thus Isaiah hopes for Zion and in his proclamation calls the people to hope beyond the judgment.

Yet there is an important element lacking in the expectation of Isaiah. In 1.26 we heard of righteous judges and counsellors. But at another point, instead of these, there is talk of a coming king out of the house of David. In a word that according to A. Alt[15] belongs to the time after the collapse of the northern kingdom, the coming of a great light is announced to the oppressed people who dwell in the northern region, who 'walked in darkness'.

> For the yoke of his burden,
>   and the staff for his shoulder,
>   the rod of his oppressor,
>   thou hast broken as on the day of Midian.
> For every boot of the tramping warrior in battle
>   tumult
>   and every garment rolled in blood
>   will be burned as fuel for the fire. (9.4–5)

This is a message of peace. But then it immediately continues with a further proclamation:

> For to us a child is born,
>   to us a son is given;
> and the government will be upon his shoulder,
>   and his name will be called
> 'Wonderful Counsellor, Mighty God,
>   Everlasting Father, Prince of Peace'.
> Of the increase of his government and of peace
>   there will be no end,
>   upon the throne of David, and over his kingdom,
>   to establish it, and to uphold it
> with justice and with righteousness
>   from this time forth and for evermore. (9.6–7)

In these words there appear elements of old coronation rituals such as are frequently found in Egypt: the identification of the new king as a child, the son of God, the bestowal of new royal names, the statements about the power and righteousness of the king. That such an expectation of a new and righteous king is part of Isaiah's vision of hope is further confirmed by 11.1ff., where there is mention of the shoot that will come forth from the stump of Jesse. Here also there is first a reference to judgment, to the felling of a tree. But out of the root, from which the monarchy of David descended (Jesse is the father of David), a ruler will spring up anew.

> And the Spirit of Yalweh shall rest upon him,
>   the spirit of wisdom and understanding,
>   the spirit of counsel and might,

> the spirit of knowledge and the fear of Yahweh . . .
> with righteousness he shall judge the poor,
> and decide with equity for the meek of the earth . . .

It is not undisputed as to whether the continuation, which speaks of the extension of peace to the animal world, belongs to what has gone before:

> The wolf shall dwell with the lamb,
> and the leopard shall lie down with the kid,
> and the calf and the lion and the fatling together,
> and a little child shall lead them.
> The cow and bear shall feed;
> their young shall lie down together;
> and the lion shall eat straw like the ox.
> The sucking child shall play over the hole of the asp,
> and the weaned child shall put his hand on the adder's
> den.

It is also disputed as to whether the words of 2.2–5, which appear also in Micah 4.1–4, and which speak of the extension of peace throughout the human world without identifying a king but only Zion and the Lord who dwells in the sanctuary there, originate with the proclamation of Isaiah. It could well be an extension of his thought, formulated perhaps by his disciples, that we have in the words about a great pilgrimage of the peoples to the holy mountain in which one people encourages the other:

> 'Come, let us go up to the mountain of Yahweh,
> to the house of the God of Jacob;
> that he may teach us his ways
> and that we may walk in his paths.'
> For out of Zion shall go forth the law,
> and the word of Yahweh from Jerusalem.

And then the consequences of this instruction are described:

> They shall beat their swords into ploughshares,
> and their spears into pruning hooks;
> nation shall not lift up sword against nation,
> neither shall they learn war any more.

Whatever may be the case with the origins of this expansion of the proclamation of peace into natural history and universal history, it is certainly clear that, behind all Isaiah's announcements of judgment and death and an end, there is in his proclamation an expectation of coming divine salvation and the creation of peace and righteousness. In his expectation of a king under whom peace would become reality, he is near to Micah, from whom on the other hand he differs sharply in his expectation that it will depend on a descendant of David and an event in Jerusalem on Mount Zion. But both Judean prophets are united in the formulation of their expectation in contrast to that of Hosea, who saw at the end a new period of wilderness wandering and, following upon this, a new possession of the land.

In this connection it is clear today that Hosea, Micah, and Isaiah inhabited various spheres of tradition:[16] the north Israelite Hosea who lives in the world of the early Israelite amphictyonic tradition of the Exodus and wilderness wanderings in contrast with Isaiah, the Jerusalem citizen in whom survive the perhaps already Canaanite traditions of Zion and the traditions of the early monarchy derived from those of David. From this kind of inquiry many worthwhile and valuable observations have been made which sharply outline the individual profile of the prophets. But we must not lose sight of what is most decisive for their proclamation, that Hosea and Micah as also Isaiah do not simply desire to re-activate older traditions, but that the prophet with all the peculiarities of his outlook, peculiarities which illuminate the origins of his speech, is above all one who is grasped by God and sent by him with the word of Yahweh's judgment and redemption of his people. It is a question of the confrontation of the people of God with their God, the 'Holy One of Israel', as Isaiah calls Yahweh. That Yahweh's intention is fulfilled against all other powers, this is the heart of the matter.

> For Yahweh of hosts has purposed,
> 　　and who will annul it?
> His hand is stretched out,
> 　　and who will turn it back? (14.27)

This God whom he encountered in Jerusalem in the temple in such a way that in his presence the prophet almost went under, and who then through the seraphim purged his lips and gave him new life – this God and his coming are what Isaiah was constrained to announce to the people. The word that this God, the Holy One of Israel, was determined to remain Israel's God through all the fires of judgment and acknowledged himself in faithfulness to his chosen Temple, Zion, and to his chosen king, David, provides the reason why Isaiah's proclamation too is not without the promise of future and hope. But here also hope and the future rest with God's faithful action which man receives in returning and faith, and before which he must give up all of the other securities of this world.

NOTES

[1] Cf. also e.g. M. Noth, *History of Israel,* 2nd ed. revised (London 1960), pp. 255ff.

[2] A. Weiser, *Das Buch der zwölf Kleinen Propheten* I (ATD 24⁴, 1963), pp. 127–206; T. H. Robinson, *Die zwölf Kleinen Propheten* (HAT 14², 1954), pp. 70–108; H. W. Wolff, *Dodekapropheton* (BKAT 14.2, 1967ff.), pp. 105ff.; J. L. Mays, *Amos* (OTL, 1969).

[3] H. Gressmann, *Der Ursprung der israelitisch-jüdischen Eschatologie* (FRLANT 6, 1905), pp. 141ff.

[4] G. von Rad, *Old Testament Theology* II, pp. 130–8. esp. p. 137.

[5] The word here is not to be attributed to Amos, as in Wolff, *op. cit.,* p. 133, but to 'his earliest disciples'.

[6] Weiser, *op. cit.,* pp. 11–104; T. H. Robinson, *op. cit.,* pp. 1–54; H. W. Wolff, *Dodekapropheton* (BKAT 14.1, 1961); J. L. Mays, *Hosea* (OTL, 1969).

[7] A. Alt, 'Hosea 5.8–6.6. Ein Krieg und seine Folgen in prophetischer Beleuchtung', *Neue kirchliche Zeitschrift* 30 (1919), pp. 537–68 (=*KlSchr* II, pp. 163–87).

[8] This is an improvement on the text which reads: 'for you are not my people and I will not be yours.'

[9] Weiser, *op. cit.,* pp. 228–90; T. H. Robinson, *op. cit.,* pp. 127–52.

[10] A. Alt, 'Micha 2.1–5. *gēs anadasmos* in Juda', *Interpretationes ad Vetus Testamentum pertinentes Sigmundo Mowinckel septuagenario missae* (Oslo 1955), pp. 13–23 (=*KlSchr* III, pp. 373–81).

[11] O. Kaiser, *Der Prophet Jesaja Kapitel 1–12* (ATD 17, 1963); G. Fohrer, *Das Buch Jesaja* (Zürcher Bibelkommentare, 2 vols., Zürich 1960–62); H. Wildberger, *Jesaja* (BKAT 10, 1965ff.).

[12] Cf. also 17.12–14.

[13] Similarly also 31.4f.

[14] Herrmann, *Die Prophetischen Heilserwartung im Alten Testament*, p. 143.

[15] A. Alt, 'Jesaja 8.23–9.6. Befreiungsnacht und Krönungstag', *Festschrift A. Bertholet zum 80. Geburtstag gewidmet* (Tübingen 1950), pp. 29–49 (=*KlSchr* II, pp. 206–25).

[16] E. Rohland, *Die Bedeutung der Erwählungstraditionen Israels für die Eschatologie der alttestamentlichen Propheten* (Diss. Heidelberg, 1956). Also G. von Rad, *Old Testament Theology* II, *passim.*

VIII

THE PROPHECY OF THE LAST YEARS OF
JUDAH AND THE BEGINNING OF THE
PERIOD OF THE EXILE

THE prophets of the initial period of Assyrian political dominance
in Syria-Palestine entered this period with images of expectation
which took a variety of forms. But history appeared to prove all
these expectations to be nothing but empty illusions. With a heavy
foot the Assyrian military rule trampled upon all these hopes and
dictated its own law to the dazed lands. The living word of God
appeared to bow before this dictation. Throughout a long half
century, the first half of the seventh century and even far into the
second half, no report of any prophetic word remains to us.

This is the time of King Manasseh, the son of Hezekiah, under
whom Isaiah had preached. This ruler followed strictly and with
determination the political policy of submission to the Assyrians
and evidently clamped down with an iron hand to prevent any
other voice from being heard within his jurisdiction during the
fifty-five years of his reign – the longest reign of any king of
Judah. When II Kings 21.16 says: 'Moreover Manasseh shed very
much innocent blood, till he had filled Jerusalem from one end to
another,' we might ask whether the blood of prophets is not included in this innocent blood, whether they were not silenced by
force. In the prophets' very general condemnation in II Kings
21.10–15, announcing the destruction of Jerusalem because of the
sins of Manasseh, no prophets are mentioned by name.

This first changes as Assyria begins to decline and finally in
quite a short period falls from its exalted position, subsequently
disappearing from the scene completely without even experiencing
a partial recovery. This sudden fall from the loftiest heights into
nothing is proclaimed an act of the judgment of Yahweh by the

prophecy of Nahum,[1] who directed his word especially against the capital of Assyria, Nineveh. This word of judgment is, however, a word of redemption for Judah, whom the prophet summons in 1.15; 2.2 with the words:

> Behold, on the mountains the feet of him
>   who brings good tidings,
>   who proclaims peace!
> Keep your feasts, O Judah,
>   fulfil your vows,
> for never again shall the wicked come against you,
>   he is utterly cut off.
> For Yahweh is restoring the majesty [or originally:
>   the vineyard?] of Jacob
>   as the majesty of Israel.

Thus does Nahum see the living God at work on behalf of his people.

But soon after this unexpected interlude of apparent new independence for Judah under Josiah, the Babylonians take the place of the Assyrians. Their coming is announced in the words of Habakkuk[2]. The Chaldeans are seen here as sent from God. God had sent them to battle against the wicked and violent man (this is understood as a reference to the representatives of Assyria). In a significant elaboration of God's decree for which the prophet is writing, there is expressed what real salvation means in such a period of confusion and danger. The divine decree (2.4) says that the righteous shall remain alive through his faithfulness to God. The psalm in chapter 3, which should perhaps be viewed as a prophetic liturgy, betrays the same hopeful point of view. It describes the powerful intervention of Yahweh in battle against the people of the oppressor.

> Thou wentest forth for the salvation of thy people,
>   for the salvation of thy anointed. (3.13)

In such knowledge of the redemptive intervention of God the worshipper dares to rejoice in the 'God of my salvation' even in the midst of his terror at the approach of God (3.18).

If we hear in Nahum as in Habakkuk the recognition of the redemptive act of Yahweh on behalf of his people, then the prophetic proclamation of Zephaniah,[3] dating probably from the earlier days of King Josiah, reminds us of the prophets of judgment of earlier years. As in Amos and Isaiah, but more impressively elaborated, we are told here of the great 'Day of Yahweh' that will bring the judgment of God upon the land and above all upon Jerusalem. The medieval 'Dies irae, dies illa, solvet saeclum in favilla' is an echo of Zeph. 1–2. It may well be reminiscent of Amos, but also of Isaiah as in connection with the description of the 'day of wrath', it says:

> Seek the Lord, all you humble of the land,
>   who do his commands;
> seek righteousness, seek humility;
>   perhaps you may be hidden
>   on the day of the wrath of Yahweh. (Zeph. 2.3)

The announcement of the destruction of everything exalted and proud is made concrete, as in Isaiah, by a reference to the remnant:

> For I will leave in the midst of you
>   a people humble and lowly.
> They shall seek refuge in the name of Yahweh,
>   those who are left in Israel;
> they shall do no wrong
>   and utter no lies,
> nor shall there be found in their mouth
>   a deceitful tongue.
> For they shall pasture and lie down,
>   and none shall make them afraid. (Zeph. 3.12f.)

In the preservation of such a remnant that will cling to God in humility lies Israel's only hope. But here also we hear the 'perhaps' of Amos, which reserves to God complete freedom.

But the great prophetic figure who shared in and suffered with the last decade of Judah, which issued in the collapse of the state, the destruction of Jerusalem and its temple, is the prophet Jeremiah[4] from the little village of Anathoth, a little north of Jerusalem.

If we may trust the statement of the book bearing his name, Jeremiah while young in years is called to be a prophet in the thirteenth year of the King Josiah, that is, in the year 627/6. He lived on after 622, the period of Deuteronomic reform, through the transition to the sphere of Egyptian domination after the death of Josiah at Megiddo, which however soon came to an end in 605/4 with the invasion of Syria-Palestine by Nebuchadnezzar. There follow the years of the state's fluctuating fortunes under the successors of Josiah, leading at the beginning of the year 597 to the first punitive reaction of the Babylonians and the deportation of the upper classes of the land, and then in 587 to complete collapse. The last narratives in the book show that, in connection with further disturbances accompanying the murder of Gedaliah, the Jewish governor installed by Babylon, the prophet is taken to Egypt by a group of refugees. There we lose all trace of him.

The message proclaimed by Jeremiah during these politically stormy years is one of overwhelming consistency. In the initial years before the reform period he announces the invasion of a sinister enemy from the north. An identification of this enemy, characterized by such indefinite outlines, with the Scythians, whose invasion of Syria-Palestine is reported by Herodotus, is more than uncertain.[5] During the period of reform Jeremiah appears to have kept silent. He neither spoke against the reform nor supported it. But after the death of Josiah he appears again on the scene with his proclamation. Subsequently he clearly sees in the invasion of the Babylonians from the north an enemy sent by God against his people. Thus he can simply identify their king Nebuchadnezzar as a 'servant of Yahweh'. And he does not budge from this line of proclamation as resistance to Babylon begins to develop in the land. Even in the last desperate battle against the Babylonians, when he himself is arrested and thrown into the court of the guard, he does not tire of calling for subjection to the enemy appointed by God and therefore to the judgment of God. The siren voices who proclaim Egypt, the counterpoise to the Babylonian rule, as a possible ally and deliverer from the Babylonian yoke, always meet with his vigorous opposition.

But the proclamation of Jeremiah takes its characteristic lines from another direction. In a quite unique fashion it becomes apparent that the prophet himself with his whole being is drawn as a fellow-sufferer into the trouble that he announces. Even in the early words about the enemy from the north one senses how the terror that this sinister and gruesome enemy creates in the prophet's people overwhelms him also and even affects him physically.

> My anguish, my anguish! I writhe in pain!
>   O, the walls of my heart!
> My heart is beating wildly;
>   I cannot keep silent;
> for I hear the sound of the trumpet,
>   the alarm of war.

> Disaster follows hard on disaster,
>   the whole land is laid waste.
> Suddenly my tents are destroyed,
>   my curtains in a moment.
> How long must I see the standard (raised),
>   and hear the sound of the trumpet? (Jer. 4.19–21)

This continues to be the case. Quite the most remarkable section of the book of Jeremiah consists of the so-called confessions of the prophet. In the style of the psalm of lamentation he presents his complaints to God in the words inserted between chs. 11 and 20 when the words of Jeremiah were collected – complaints that can intensify to the point of sharp indictment of God and which speak not only of the fate of the people but also the very personal suffering of the prophet in the ministry of opposition that is inwardly and outwardly part of his office. In all this his resistance to his task, already evident in the report of his call, in no way frees him from his office.

> If I say, 'I will not mention him,
>   or speak any more in his name,'
> there is in my heart as it were a burning fire
>   shut up in my bones,
> and I am weary with holding it in,
>   and I cannot. (Jer. 20.9)

With no other prophet is the inescapable character of the task laid upon him so clearly discernible as with Jeremiah. At the same time one senses into how deep a night the prophet is cast because of this inescapable aspect. In the last of the confessions it reaches the point of a curse on the day he was born, which prefigures the words of Job 3.

> Cursed be the day
>   on which I was born!
> The day when my mother bore me,
>   let it not be blessed!
> Cursed be the man
>   who brought the news to my father,
> 'A son is born to you,'
>   making him very glad.
> Let that man be like the cities
>   which Yahweh overthrew without pity;

> let him hear a cry in the morning
> and an alarm at noon,
> because he did not kill me in the womb;
> so my mother would have been my grave,
> and her womb for ever great.
> Why did I come forth from the womb
> to see toil and sorrow,
> and spend my days in shame? (Jer. 20.14–18)

It is in order here to ask if we can detect any sign of hope and of a future behind what Jeremiah says in his message. To deal with this we must mention a peculiar difficulty that the book of Jeremiah presents. It has always been obvious that many sections of this book contain statements whose style exhibits a markedly Deuteronomistic colouring. This includes not only the narrative material but also a whole series of the speeches of Jeremiah. S. Herrmann[6] has attempted to demonstrate that in many salvation pronouncements of the book of Jeremiah a conception of salvation is expressed in which salvation is not announced prophetically but is offered as an alternative to the individual and the nation: If a man will turn from his evil ways, will hear the voice of Yahweh, will do good, will seek Yahweh with his whole heart, then salvation will be given him. If he does not do this, then he can expect trouble. From this point of view one can even detect in Jeremiah 1 penetration of the story of the call of Jeremiah, whose struggle against his office is also clearly seen here, by a kind of scheme:

> See, I have set you this day over nations and over kingdoms,
> to pluck up and to break down,
> to destroy and to overthrow,
> to build and to plant. (Jer. 1.10)

In the prophet's direct proclamation where we are undoubtedly confronted with his original words, this didactic scheme apparently does not exist. This is not to say that here nothing is said about hope for a redemptive future. Statements that expressly use the vocabulary established earlier for hope and hoping, can be found in any case in statements by the people which find an echo in the book of the prophet. As in Hosea, so here, we meet the phenomenon of sections of liturgical character in which the prophetic word is a response to the people's psalm-like prayers and lamentations.

In a great 'day of repentance' liturgy in a time of drought one hears the complaint of the people:

> We looked (*qwh*) for peace, but no good came;
>   for a time of healing, but behold, terror. (Jer. 14.19b)

The first half of the sentence appears word for word in 8.15. 13.16 speaks of futile waiting (*qwh*) for light. In view of this absence of salvation the people declare:

> Are there any among the false gods of the nations that can bring rain?
>   Or can the heavens give showers?
> Art thou not he, Yahweh our God?
>   We set our hope (*qwh*) on thee. (Jer. 14.22)

Only in the book of Jeremiah of all the prophetic writings do we find the substantive identification of Yahweh as *miqweh*, 'object of trust' for Israel. The setting appears to be the confession of trust found in the prayer of the people as they call on God:

> O thou hope of Israel,
>   its saviour in time of trouble . . . (Jer. 14.8)

> Yahweh, the hope of Israel,
>   all who forsake thee shall be put to shame. (17.13)

In 50.7, a saying that admittedly is only later ascribed to Jeremiah, Yahweh is identified with the same word *miqweh* as 'their Father of hope'. Both the other examples of the use of *miqweh*, Ezra 10.2 and I Chron. 29.15, are also found in prayers.

The prophet responds to this hopeful expectation in the liturgies both of 14.1–15.4 and also of 3.21–4.4 with sharp rejection and the pronouncement of judgment. But it is clear that in another context he is able to speak of a redemptive future. The compositions in 3.6ff. and chs. 30f., which we will look at first here, are both from the time of Josiah according to their superscriptions. Even if this may not hold for all the prophetic words collected here, it is true for individual sections of these passages. According to the historical reports available to us, the reform of Josiah had evidently extended into the Assyrian provinces to the north, the area of the earlier northern kingdom. It is in this context that the demonstrable birth of new hope for this area not only in Jeremiah, but also in Ezekiel should be understood. Therefore in Jer. 3.12f. the call of invitation to the north is to be heard:

> Return, faithless Israel, says Yahweh.
> I will not look on you in anger,
>   for I am merciful, says Yahweh;
> I will not be angry for ever.
> Only acknowledge your guilt,
>   that you rebelled against Yahweh your God.

Here the mercy of God, in which Yahweh identifies himself as uniquely *hasid*, covenant-faithful, appears anew for the apparently lost Israel in the north. And to this come words from chapter 31 which dare to speak openly of hope:

> A voice is heard in Ramah,
>   lamentation and bitter weeping.
> Rachel is weeping for her children;
>   she refuses to be comforted for her children,
>   because they are not.
> Thus says Yahweh:
> 'Keep your voice from weeping
>   and your eyes from tears;
> for your work shall be rewarded,' says Yahweh,
>   'and they shall come back from the land of the enemy.
> There is hope (*tiqwāh*) for your future,' says Yahweh,
>   'and your children shall come back to their own
>   country.' (31.15–17)

Did Jeremiah also allow Judah and Jerusalem such a future hope? In individual cases of admonition in his earlier writings one may hear such an offer hidden behind the exhortations, as for example in 4.14:

> O Jerusalem, wash your heart from wickedness,
>   that you may be saved.
> How long shall your evil thoughts
>   lodge within you?

We find similar ideas in 4.3f. and 6.8. Seen from this vantage point the double 'perhaps' of 36.3 and 7, formulated by another hand, may be seen to coincide with Jeremiah's own opinion. Jeremiah 36 relates how Baruch is sent with the scroll dictated by Jeremiah to the temple, where the people are holding a day of repentance, in order to read these words there: 'It may be that their supplication will come before Yahweh and that every one will turn from his evil way' . . . so that what God had previously said about the purport of the words of judgment written in the scroll might become true:

> It may be that the house of Judah will hear all the evil which I intend to do to them, so that every one may turn from his evil way, and that I may forgive their iniquity and their sin. (Jer.36.3)

In another place we seem to encounter undoubted promises of a future and of hope for Judah also. In the first days of the year 597, just after the first invasion of Nebuchadnezzar, a not insignificant group of notable men of the country are deported to Babylon. In ch. 24, which was undoubtedly formulated by the Deuteronomist, a picture is drawn of two fig baskets filled with good and bad figs, which the prophet then identifies as those who remain behind and those who are led away. Here it is apparent that he sees the future, as does Ezekiel of Judah also in a different way, preserved in those who have been deported. In light of this one must seriously question whether the passage 29.10–14, which has been inserted into the letter of Jeremiah to the exiles, does not, in spite of its Deuteronomistic phraseology, contain the substance of Jeremiah's words to these deported, especially where we read: '"I know the plans I have for you," says Yahweh, "plans for welfare and not for evil, to give you a future and a hope (*'aḥᵃrīt wᵉ tiqwāh*)."' That Jeremiah expects this future to be a future in the land of promise is especially clear from what we read in Jer. 32, again, to be sure, in Deuteronomistic phraseology, but undoubtedly reliable so far as the event here reported is concerned. In the midst of the siege of Jerusalem, when Jeremiah is already imprisoned in the court of the guard, Yahweh announces to him the coming of a relative, Hanamel, who will offer Jeremiah, as the nearest relative with first chance at it, the opportunity to buy a field in Anathoth, land already occupied by the enemy. On the basis of Yahweh's promise, Jeremiah buys the land even on the eve of a catastrophe that he himself has proclaimed as inevitable and takes great care that the deed of sale with the signature of witnesses is well preserved. The word of Yahweh that comes to him through this apparently senseless purchase is this: 'Houses and fields and vineyards shall again be bought in this land' (Jer. 32.15). But this is a definite pledge of a future and of hope beyond the judgment which threatens unavoidably even at that very hour.

At two points it may be possible to make this expectation some-what more concrete. In part of a collection of sayings under the superscription: 'Of the house of the King of Judah' (Jer. 21.11) we hear in 23.5f. a word that comes again in a slightly different form in 33.15f.

Behold, the days are coming, says Yahweh, when I will raise up for David a righteous Branch, and he shall reign as king and deal wisely and shall execute justice and righteousness in the land. In his days Judah will be saved, and Israel will dwell securely. And this is the name by which he will be called: 'The Lord is our righteousness.'

It is possible that the prophet, at a time when the Egyptian inva-sion had interrupted the true royal succession, takes up the ancient promise to the house of David of a future for the lawful Davidic monarchy. To be sure the reference to this special future for the monarchy does not appear again in the words handed down to us. Undoubtedly it does not possess the weight in the proclamation of Jeremiah that it has in Isaiah.

It is much disputed whether the significant word in the little book of salvation, chs. 30f., which opens up a view of a new covenant between God and his people, is part of the proclamation of Jeremiah or whether, as Herrmann holds,[7] it sets forth later Deuteronomistic covenant theology. Here there is talk of a coming new formation of the people of God in a new covenant, which will supplant the old covenant established after the Exodus from Egypt. According to this new covenant the commandment of God will be written in the hearts of his people, so that no one will need to teach anyone else or say to him, 'Know the Lord' for they will all know Yahweh from the least to the greatest and he will forgive their sin and iniquity (31.31–34). Here a day is seen in which the threat to Israel issuing from its disobedience will come to an end, because it will willingly know and acknowledge God's command.

However wide one may draw the circle enclosing statements of hope formulated by Jeremiah himself, it is in any case clear that this prophet, so marked by suffering and in his oppression entering into dispute with his God, again and again experienced the en-couragement of his God who promised him deliverance from his distress – we hear it in the confession of 15.15–21, in which the declaration of the sweetness of God's word ('Thy words were found, and I ate them, and thy words became to me a joy and the

delight of my heart; for I am called by thy name') stands next to
the complaint about the loneliness and isolation that this very word
has laid upon him and in which God himself must call the prophet
to repentance for his strong attacks upon God's evil dealings.
Here the reprimand of God issues in a very personal promise:
'. . . "I am with you to save you and deliver you," says Yahweh'
(v. 20). Through this promise which appears also in the account of
the prophet's call in 1.8 and 19, the prophet knows that God is
with him in his darkest affliction and promises him a future. Thus
we further see that Jeremiah is for his part empowered to promise
deliverance and a future to other individuals in very specific situations: in 35.19 it is a group of Rechabites, whose faithfulness to
the laws of their ancestors had impressed him; in 39.17f. it is the
Cushite, Ebedmelech, who had saved his life; and in 45.5 it is his
faithful friend and helper, Baruch, who like Jeremiah is threatened
with the same exposure to persecution and legal proceedings.

Somewhat in contrast to Isaiah, there is in Jeremiah very little
in the way of major projections of expectation toward the future.
But there lives in the proclamation of this prophet, in his anxiety
and distress, himself inwardly shaken by the judgment he preached,
the knowledge that God, even today where he appears to act in
pure judgment, is on the march to guide into the future.

Next to Jeremiah we must consider Ezekiel.[8] According to the
introductory words of his book he was called to be a prophet in
the summer of 593, more than thirty years after Jeremiah, and
after he had experienced, with the upper strata of society and
Jehoiachin's entourage, the deportation to Babylon at the beginning
of the year 597. There he lived with a group of exiles at a place not
far from the southern Babylonian city of Nippur, that apparently
as the site of a settlement long deserted had the name *tēl'ābīb*, 'hill
of the flood'.

In this prophet's message, which he presents in part in striking
symbolic acts, there is in the foreground, so far as we can tell, the
announcement of the imminent and final fall of the city of Jerusalem which had been spared in the year 597. Chapter 7 sternly
presents the message using the catch-word given by Amos, 'The
end has come!' At the same time we see how Ezekiel, working
with broadly developed general historical outlines, takes away
from his people every possibility of pride and makes clear their
sinful corruption at its very roots. Using the marriage picture of

Hosea and Jeremiah, ch. 16 describes the city of Jerusalem, and ch. 23 the two kingdoms of the pre-exilic monarchical period, in pictures of one, then two women, corrupted from youth, who are unfaithful to their legitimate husband, Yahweh. Ezek. 20 describes without imagery how Israel, even as early as the time which the credal statements and also Hosea and Jeremiah paint in glowing colours as the good times of beginnings, was an evil and repeatedly rebellious people for whom Yahweh even in this initial period had to contemplate the punishment of exile. In all this Ezekiel becomes the stern consummation of radical accusation and of the message of judgment upon his people. It is not surprising that from a people addressed like this at a time when destruction had run its full course, there came words of despair rejecting all hope. In Ezek. 37.11 we hear: 'Our bones are dried up, and our hope (*tiqwāh*) is lost; we are clean cut off.' And in the word quoted in 33.10, the knowledge of individual guilt engulfs in despair those responsible: 'Our transgressions and our sins are upon us, and we waste away because of them; how then can we live?' This is the appropriate reaction to the proclamation of the prophet: for an Israel so radically sinful, there can no longer be life, hope or future.

But then it is surprising to find that it was none other than Ezekiel who became the proclaimer of a new future, who by his proclamation undoubtedly helped at a crucial point to prevent the collapse of the people lost in exile and to turn them to face a new future.

If we ask about the first appearance of the proclamation of a future in Ezekiel – and here I must differ with S. Herrmann's opinion that this proclamation should be attributed to later written elaborations by the prophet's disciples – then the setting of Ezek. 36.16ff. may give us the clearest explanation. Here there is first of all another reference back to Israel's history of transgression which terminates in the dispersion of the people throughout other lands. This is described as the history of the profanation of the name of God. Yahweh himself, who had bound himself to this people by his name, was profaned among the peoples in this history because the peoples among whom the Israelites are dispersed can say: 'These are the people of Yahweh, and yet they had to go out of his land.' So it is the honour of the divine name that provides the particular grounds for the intervention of Yahweh in which he again gives his people a future and a hope:

'It is not for your sake, O house of Israel, that I am about to act, but for the sake of my holy name, which you have profaned among the nations to which you came. And I will vindicate the holiness of my great name, which has been profaned among the nations and which you have profaned among them; and the nations will know that I am Yahweh,' says Yahweh. (36.22f.)

Here it is not burning love in the heart of Yahweh, as in Hosea, which simply cannot punish any longer. It is not as in Isaiah a reference to the faithfulness of Yahweh to his holy city or the Davidic line chosen by him, but rather it is the majesty and honour of God himself, in which having once attached his name to the people of Israel, his people, he does not take it back, but rather through the resurrection of Israel restores to his name its honour. This cannot remain a hidden act. The peoples must recognize that Yahweh is acting in all this and is making himself known in his authentic being to the world. In Ezekiel this formula for recognition often presents itself in a variety of forms.[9] In all the acts of God knowledge of Yahweh is what matters, in his activity of judgment which reveals the fire of his holiness no less than in his acts of new creation.

It is very clear in the vision of 37.1ff. that here in this act of Yahweh we are in fact confronted with a new creation of the dead. Here the prophet is transported to a field full of dead bones which are completely bleached and dried up. There he hears the command to prophesy over these bones, that is, by the command of Yahweh to call them to life. Then a rustling begins among the bones:

. . . the bones came together, bone to its bone. And as I looked, there were sinews on them, and flesh had come upon them, and skin had covered them; but there was no breath in them. (37.7f.)

Then the prophet is called a second time to prophesy and to summon breath:

So I prophesied as he commanded me, and the breath came into them, and they lived, and stood upon their feet, an exceedingly great host. (37.10)

And then the meaning of this uncanny event is disclosed to the prophet. It contains the promise of Yahweh to Israel:

Behold, I will open your graves, and raise you from your graves, O my people, and I will bring you home into the land of Israel . . . And I will put my Spirit within you, and you shall live, and I will place you in your own land; then you shall know that I, Yahweh, have spoken, and I have done it, says Yahweh. (37.12, 14)

It is clear that in this vision the prophet is not being given information about individual resurrection of the dead. It is a matter here of the people of God and its resurrection out of the death caused by its sin. The despairing congregation of God, which says, 'Our bones are dried up, our hope is gone', shall learn hope – not because there is yet life in it, but because God promises that he is yet at work in it and will awaken it to life even as he once at the beginning, according to Gen. 2.7, formed the body as its Creator and breathed the breath of life into that dead body.

In ch. 36, which has a parallel in 11.14–21, this is extended to man's inner being. God will cleanse his people and give them a new heart and a new spirit for their inner life, will take away their stony hearts and give them hearts of flesh. This is reminiscent of the statement in Jer. 31 which says that the law of God will be written on the hearts of his people.

Besides these great promises dealing with the categories of the new creation of the future of God's people and the renewal of its devastated land, there are also in Ezekiel sayings which link up with the earlier prophets. He reminds us of Hosea, when in 20.32ff. he speaks of a new exodus out of the peoples, a new movement through the desert where God will meet his people face to face in a judgment of purging, then to lead those who survive into the land. We are reminded of Isaiah and Micah when in ch. 34, after reproachful words against the evil shepherds, he talks of the good flock and the appointment of David, the servant of God, as the one good shepherd over the people. The reference to the coming king of God is perhaps discernible also in 17.22–24. But there emerges even more strongly, in Ezekiel's statements about the future, a reference to the new sanctuary upon the holy mountain of Israel. According to ch. 20 this is the point where the new exodus and the new leading into the land really end. 37.27f. also promises:

My dwelling place shall be with them, and I will be their God, and they shall be my people. Then the nations will know that I Yahweh sanctify Israel, when my sanctuary is in the midst of them for evermore.

This is above all the theme recognizable in the massive final vision of chs. 40–48, whose development also undoubtedly involved the work of other hands. Here the prophet, who has been carried off to Jerusalem, sees upon the holy mountain the new sanctuary erected in absolutely pure symmetry. He gazes as the glory of God invades the sanctuary. According to chs. 8–11 he had seen in a corresponding vision how God had left his temple and had allowed fire to race through the city. From this place of the presence of God, this 'place of my throne and the place of the soles of my feet, where I will dwell in the midst of the people of Israel for ever', as 43.7 phrases it, there flows into the land, according to 47.1–12, a stream of water at first very small, but then ever greater, there to heal even the sick Dead Sea, so that fish begin to play there.

From the imagery of these representations may be drawn the great promise that the decisive event will be that God will once again dwell in the midst of his people, and that this will cause everything else to be set right. It is unmistakably clear that this expectation is very similar to that of the priestly writings with their historicizing reflection and its unmistakable element of expectation, which bases the fullest hope, which enables the people of God to step out with confidence toward their future, upon the fact that God has promised to come to them and remain in their midst for all time.

It is also true of Ezekiel that, in this entire vision of the future, the word 'hope' is never used. Where it is used, as in 37.11; 19.5 it is used to look back at situations of hopelessness. But the substance of hope and of a future is fully there as the prophet announces the coming activity of his God. Here also in Ezekiel all authentic hope rests with the promise and pledge of God.

Under the impact of this prophetic statement in the night of exile the miracle happens: a despairing people are renewed to become a people of expectation and finally a people moving confidently into a future of deliverance. This is seen more fully in the other prophet of the exile, Second Isaiah.

NOTES

[1] K. Elliger, *Das Buch der zwölf Kleinen Propheten* II (ATD 25⁵, 1964), pp. 1–22; F. Horst, *Die zwölf Kleinen Propheten* (HAT 14², 1954), pp. 153–66.

[2] Elliger, *op. cit.,* pp. 23–55; Horst, *op. cit.,* pp. 167–86.

[3] Elliger, *op. cit.,* pp. 56–82; Horst, *op. cit.,* pp. 187–200.

[4] A. Weiser, *Das Buch Jeremia* (ATD 20/21[5], 1966); W. Rudolph, *Jeremia* (HAT 12[3], 1968).

[5] Herodotus I, 103–6.

[6] Herrmann, *Die prophetischen Heilserwartung*, pp. 159ff.

[7] Herrmann, *ibid.*, pp. 179–85.

[8] W. Eichrodt, *Ezekiel* (OTL, 1970); G. Fohrer and K. Galling, *Ezechiel* (HAT 13, 1955); W. Zimmerli, *Ezechiel* (BKAT 13, 1955ff.).

[9] W. Zimmerli, *Erkenntnis Gottes nach dem Buche Ezechiel. Eine theologische Studie* (ATANT 27, 1954) (=*Gottes Offenbarung*, ThB 19, 1963, pp. 41–119).

IX

SECOND ISAIAH
AND THE LAST OF WRITTEN PROPHECY

At the beginning of the period of the Judean exile stands Ezekiel, whose proclamation binds together the stern 'no' to the possibility of the old life with the announcement of the resurrection of the dead to new life through God himself. At the end of the exilic period there stands the proclamation of Second Isaiah, whose words are found in Isaiah 40–55.[1] Through his words there echoes jubilation over the hour of redemption which stands right at the door. As a great proclamation of certain hope everything in this message presses toward the future of impending redemption.

To the question of the basis for this powerful proclamation of a future, the prophet does not remain silent. It was evidently made clear to him even at the moment of his call. The word of 40.6–8, a word embedded in a thematic introductory group of sayings, directs us to this moment. According to this word a voice summoned the prophet with the demand, 'Proclaim!' To his puzzled counter-question: 'What shall I proclaim?' comes the answer:

> All flesh is grass,
>> and all its beauty is like the flower of the field.
> The grass withers, the flower fades . . .
>> but the word of our God will stand for ever.

Here in a thesis that appears almost dualistic, there is first a reference to that which in a world marked by existential transitoriness alone has a future (the statement reminds us of Job and Lamentations). The saying in 55.10f., which is deliberately placed in the concluding collection of sayings by the redactors of the entire book, clearly demonstrates that this impression of a dualistic opposition between the world of transitoriness and the world of God's word is false. When we hear:

For as the rain and the snow come down from heaven,
    and return not thither but water the earth,
making it bring forth and sprout,
    giving seed to the sower and bread to the eater,
so shall my word be that goes forth from my mouth;
    it shall not return to me empty,
but it shall accomplish that which I purpose,
    and prosper in the thing for which I sent it,

it is clear that in this word God turns to his world in such a way that whoever lives in this world of the transitory can come to know a future and a hope in the encounter with this word at work. What is audible here in thematic words at beginning and end also completely pervades the rest of the prophet's proclamation.

It is easy to see that Second Isaiah takes up earlier prophetic words in his proclamation and declares their effectiveness in his immediate present. As early as Hosea it was said that Yahweh would lead his people through a new wilderness period to new redemption. In Ezek. 20.32ff. this announcement has developed in a much more broadly elaborated word which spoke of a new deliverance from among the nations, a new wilderness wandering with a judgment and purgation, and a new leading into the land.[2] This proclamation of a new wilderness journey toward Zion now dominates Second Isaiah's message. In contrast to Ezek. 20, it is not developed here in a thoroughly consistent picture. In conformity with Second Isaiah's sweeping, never pedantic, style of proclamation, this new future is illuminated as if by flash-light in bursts of individual words, which then are preserved for the most part in the category of oracles of hearing.[3] In these, as we gather from the announcements of salvation by Second Isaiah, every reference to a visible event of punishment in the wilderness drops out. With the picture of a wilderness journey marked with glory, in which Yahweh himself leads his people with the care of a good shepherd (Isa. 40.10f.), there mingle elements of the great procession of the gods such as the exiles in their Babylonian environment must have had vividly before their eyes. Heavenly powers are bidden, as is clear already from the thematic introductory complex in 40.3–5, to build a way for Yahweh for his journey through the wilderness:

A voice cries:
'In the wilderness prepare the way of Yahweh,

make straight in the desert a highway for our God.
Every valley shall be lifted up
    and every mountain and hill be made low;
the uneven ground shall become level,
    and the rough places a plain.
And the glory of Yahweh shall be revealed,
    and all flesh shall see it together.

The typological play upon the tradition of the first wilderness journey at the beginning of the nation's history is unmistakable in Isaiah 48.20f. as the way into the new freedom is described with the words:

Yahweh has redeemed his servant Jacob!
They thirsted not when he led them through the deserts;
    he made water flow for them from the rock;
    he cleft the rock and the water gushed out.

Thus Moses once struck the rock so that water streamed out for the thirsty people to drink (Ex. 17.1–7; Num. 20.1–13). If according to the story of the first wilderness journey, the people left Egypt during the night in anxious haste, and Yahweh then led his people with a pillar of cloud by day and a pillar of fire by night (Ex. 13.21f.), protecting their rear in a moment of danger (Ex.14.20), then Isa. 52.12 announces after the prophet has called the people to depart out of the far land:

For you shall not go out in haste,
    and you shall not go in flight,
for Yahweh will go before you,
    and the God of Israel will be your rear guard.

The first of these sentences offers the further conclusion that this new Exodus is expressly presented as an Exodus far surpassing the first one. If according to Ex. 12.11 and Deut. 16.3 the passover meal indicates explicitly that the flight from Egypt was in 'anxious haste', then the second Exodus will be incomparably more glorious and will not be marked by anxiety and fearful haste. Indeed, this matter of superiority is extended further in ch. 43, in that there the command is given not to remember the former things because the new event will be so much more glorious than that earlier one. The following passage is a reminder of the wonderful deliverance at the Red Sea:

> Thus says Yahweh,
>> who makes a way in the sea,
>> a path in the mighty waters,
>> who brings forth chariot and horse,
>> army and warrior;
>> they lie down, they cannot rise,
>> they are extinguished, quenched like a wick:
> 'Remember not the former things,
>> nor consider the things of old.
> Behold, I am doing a new thing;
>> now it springs forth, do you not perceive it?
> I will make a way in the wilderness
>> and rivers in the desert.
> The wild beasts will honour me,
>> the jackals and the ostriches;
> for I give water in the wilderness,
>> rivers in the desert,
> to give drink to my chosen people,
>> the people whom I formed for myself
> that they might declare my praise.' (43.16ff.)

It would hardly be correct to interpret the proclamation here as an attack on the ancient confession of Israel, 'in words which the pious in particular must have felt to contain an element of blasphemy'.[4] It is not a polemical point of view but the thought of surpassing what went before that alone is determinative here. Before the radiance of the new, the old fades as the stars fade before the rising sun, and is no longer thought of. It is from this angle that we should understand the category of the 'new', which crops up frequently in this context. 'New things I now declare', says 42.9, to which the hymnic summons then answers, 'Sing to the Lord a new song' (42.10). This category has its origin in the language of the liturgical song of praise (cf. e.g. Pss. 33.3; 40.4; 96.1).

The journey by God's guidance back through the transformed wilderness, whose edge is bordered, according to another passage, by the most glorious and spectacular trees, cedar, acacia, myrtle, and olive (Isa. 41.19; cf. also 55.13), finds its goal in Zion where messengers of joy proclaim anew the word of the kingdom of the God of Zion. The glory of this city's foundation, battlements and gates, all made of precious stones, is described in full. Other words portray how the childless city, to its own astonishment, will suddenly become again the mother of many children, to the point that there will be a space problem for the citizens and one will say to the other: 'The place is too narrow for me; make room for me to dwell in' (49.20). For at a signal from Yahweh a movement will begin among the peoples of the world in which kings and princes will carefully bring the children of Zion back again from distant lands (49.22f.).

In the description to this point one can see how the prophetic word of God with powerful intensification actualizes anew elements of older traditions of Israel and proclaims the faithfulness of Yahweh in this new-style repetition of his original acts in the Exodus and guidance through the wilderness, and his concern for Zion. But one can see further that the prophetic proclamation at the same time with an audacious stroke dares to press forward in contemporary history toward that which is unheard of. The proclamation of the impending liberation becomes concrete as the prophet explicitly names the Persian king, Cyrus, as the saviour summoned by Yahweh for his people. It is certainly not necessary to conclude with Begrich[5] that the reference to imminent deliverance by Cyrus is the result of a definite disappointment in which the prophet recognized that a miraculous turning-point in world history transforming nature itself was not about to happen. Therefore he points realistically to the heathen ruler, Cyrus, as the one sent to deliver. Rather, the prophet's message achieves its historical concretization in the reference to Cyrus – even as in the case of Jeremiah his vague initial proclamation of an enemy from the north found its real fulfilment and confirmation in the invasion of the Neo-Babylonians.

This bold departure from all traditional expectations to point to the heathen Persian king, whose victory over the Medes and then the wealthy Croesus of Lydia had excited the world of that day, aroused in the prophet's circle, as far as we can see, not only astonishment but also opposition. He rejects this opposition with the parable originally used by Isaiah in another connection:

> Woe to him who strives with his Maker,
> an earthen vessel with the potter!
> Does the clay say to him who fashions it, 'What are
> you making?' (45.9)

Thus the announcement of Cyrus appears repeatedly against the background of the majestic reference to the creative act of Yahweh:

> 'I made the earth,
>> and created man upon it;
> it was my hands that stretched out the heavens,
>> and I commanded all their host.
> I have aroused him [that is, Cyrus] in righteousness,
>> and I will make straight all his ways;
> he shall build my city
>> and set my exiles free,
> not for price or reward,'
>> says Yahweh of hosts. (45.12f.)

In another place the appearance of Yahweh as Creator is bound up with a reference to the uniquely powerful word which Yahweh speaks through his prophets and which contrasts with the power-less word of the astrologers and fortune-tellers so common in Babylon and appearing in all such ancient cultures:

> I, Yahweh, made all things,
>> who stretched out the heavens alone,
>> who established the earth – who was with me? –
> who frustrates the omens of liars,
>> and makes fools of diviners;
> who turns wise men back,
>> and makes their knowledge foolish;
> who confirms the word of his servant,
>> and performs the counsel of his messengers;
> who says to the deep, 'Be dry,
>> I will dry up your rivers';
> who says of Cyrus, 'He is my shepherd,
>> and he shall fulfil all my purpose';
> saying of Jerusalem, 'She shall be built,
>> and I will raise up her ruins.' (Isa. 44.24–28)[6]

In the creation narrative of Genesis 1 it can be seen how the creative act of Yahweh finds its fullest expression in the mention of the word of command. There every creative act is initiated with the word of Yahweh. A similar mode of statement is recognizable in Second Isaiah also. The call of Yahweh rules everything and is a sign of the Creator's free disposition of the world and its history. Thus according to 40.26 Yahweh leads out the whole host of the stars of heaven and calls them by name, and not one dares hesitate before this call of the mighty one. And so in the same way he calls into history. After 41.1ff. has pointed to the coming of Cyrus, there follows the summary question:

> Who has performed and done this,
>   calling the generations from the beginning?
> I, Yahweh, the first,
>   and with the last; I am He. (41.4)

This majestic word of the Creator had once called forth the figure
whom Israel well knows from its own sacred history and of whom
it repeatedly speaks:

> Look to Abraham your Father [in 41.8 he receives
>   the honoured title of 'friend' of God]
> and to Sarah who bore you;
> for when he was but one I called him,
>   and I blessed him and made him many. (51.2)

But this same free creative word can also call in a completely new
way, apart from the content of the ancient tradition, as for example
when in 45.3 the God of Israel identifies himself before Cyrus as the
one 'who calls you by your name'. But this freedom can also make
possible completely new formulations of old traditional expectations and hopes without the necessity of shaking the certainty
that in his promise of a future God remains consistent with his
past.

This freedom to re-draw the concrete future expectation of
Israel is especially clear in the announcement of Cyrus.

In the earlier prophets of Judah, from Isaiah to Micah, Jeremiah
and Ezekiel, one hears the statement, in individually varied formulations, that Yahweh will appoint from the house of David or
the house of Jesse or out of Bethlehem (Beth Ephrath) the Ruler
of the coming day of redemption. Now in Isa. 45.1–7, in a gro-
tesquely expanded introductory statement about the mighty word
directed to Cyrus in which Yahweh for Israel's sake promises to
give him the kingdom and all its treasures, we read:

> Thus says Yahweh to his anointed, to Cyrus,
>   whose right hand I have grasped,
> to subdue nations before him
>   and ungird the loins of kings,
> to open doors before him
>   that gates may not be closed . . .

In deliberately provocative audacity even the title of anointed,
which in the Jerusalem tradition is already reaching the point of

becoming the exclusive designation for the expected king from the house of David, is here given to the alien and heathen Persian king, Cyrus. That this was not a solitary slip of the tongue or a momentary exuberance to be explained as mere rhetoric, can be seen from another angle in the words of Isa. 55.1-5. Here Yahweh, in the semblance of a host who calls to dinner, invites acceptance of his gift, given out of free grace:

> . . . I will make with you an everlasting covenant,
>   my steadfast, sure love for David.
> Behold, I made him a witness to the peoples,
>   a leader and commander for the peoples.
> Behold, you shall call nations that you know not,
>   and nations that knew you not shall run to you,
> because of the Lord your God, and of the Holy One of
>   Israel,
>   for he has glorified you. (vv. 3-5)

This word obviously reminds us in the first place of that promise given to David, and confirms God's faithfulness to this promise out of his own mouth. But if Israel, on the basis of earlier prophetic statements, expects the fulfilment of this promise in the person of the Davidic ruler, then here there is executed a surprising re-drawing of this expectation. The people as a whole are to participate in the promise to David. As he became a witness to the power of God through the grace given to him, so now the people as a whole are to receive this function of witness. Subsequent words of Second Isaiah develop more fully how Yahweh uses this people, blind and often oblivious to his work, as his witness in the world of the nations, a people who know how to tell of the great things that God has done among them. And if David was governor and lord of many peoples, now Israel will learn that one thing it must witness to is the approach of people out of many nations who previously had no experience of this. Isa. 44.5 describes very graphically how they will identify themselves with Israel:

> This one will say, 'I am Yahweh's',
>   another will call himself by the name of Jacob,
> and another will write on his hand, 'Yahweh's own',
>   and give himself the surname of Israel.

What has happened here? Among the events which the exiles of

Zion have directly experienced in his time, Second Isaiah recognizes that God is acting in a completely new and surprising fashion in order to make good the old promises. Through a foreign ruler and his victory over the nations, he prepares for Israel its new freedom and future. The political function of God's expected king is given over to this alien. But the central office which Israel's divinely appointed King David had and toward which the essential promise was directed, is here seen in a new and until now unknown dimension: The witness of Yahweh before all the peoples: this is the future hidden behind his promise to David, the future that God now intends for his people.

In connection with our reflection about a future and a hope according to statements of the Old Testament there is here within the prophetic writings an important phenomenon that becomes fundamentally clear. As was already evident in our consideration of the narrative works in which the priestly writings expand to new dimensions the promise to the patriarchs already reported by the Yahwist, so here within the prophetic writings a prophet opens up anew the future activity of his God. It becomes especially clear here that the prophet is not bound to a definite programme in his future expectations and does not wait for God on the basis of outward appearances and the letter of his promise, as a prophet who misunderstands God does in Jonah 4, but rather he allows himself to be led into new situations and, without vacillating, trusts God to remain faithful to his intentions.

Up to this point we have concerned ourselves primarily with the substance and content of Second Isaiah's proclamation. But beyond this concrete historical proclamation one can see that Second Isaiah expresses himself in a fundamental way, as no other prophet before him ever did, and quite apart from individual statements, about the relationship of Yahweh to history and therefore to the future of history. He does not come to this from reflection achieved by quiet contemplation detached from the context of his proclamation to his people. Rather the statements in this direction are an integral part of a proclamation that has a very definite polemical tendency. Second Isaiah lived in Babylon in a world dominated by Babylonian deities. In the face of these gods, who determined the extent of the political power of Babylon, the ultimate question of power in the world was bound to be raised. It is very significant that in the argument against the gods, it is not the problem of power in nature and creation that is the centre of concern, but the question of power in history in its past and future dimensions.[7]

In Isa. 41.4 after the announcement of Cyrus, we hear the words:

> Who has performed and done this,
>> calling the generations from the beginning?
> I, Yahweh, the first,
>> and with the last; I am He.

Again in Isa. 44.6 we hear the word:

> I am the first and I am the last;
>> besides me there is no god.

In Isa. 48.13 it becomes possible on the basis of this summary statement to refer back to the beginning, to creation itself:

> My hand laid the foundation of the earth,
>> and my right hand spread out the heavens;
> when I call to them,
>> they stand forth together.

But then the passage moves on to a reference to Cyrus as he is summoned by God and identified here as a friend of Yahweh.

It might appear here that in this summary identification of Yahweh as the first and last we are dealing in speculative and non-historical fashion with the eternal being of God. But the sharp summons with which Yahweh challenges the gods of the nations makes it immediately clear that the God of concrete historical activity is intended throughout. So in a great courtroom address (Isa. 43.8–13) in which he calls the gods before a judgment forum, he asks:

> Who among them can declare this,
>> and show us the former (first) things?
> Let them bring their witnesses to justify them,
>> and let them hear and say, It is true. (43.9)

In opposition Yahweh quotes his own witness, the people of Israel, who have experienced all his activity, and have come to know how what he proclaimed through his prophets has been confirmed by history:

'You are my witnesses,' says Yahweh,
   'and my servant whom I have chosen,
that people may know and believe me
   and understand that I am He.
Before me no god was formed,
   nor shall there be any after me.' (43.10)[8]

In the judgment of 41.21–29 in which Yahweh summons the gods to court, we hear the words:

'Set forth your case,' says Yahweh;
   'bring your proofs,' says the King of Jacob.

Then follow a whole flood of challenges with which Yahweh attacks the gods of the nations:

Tell us the former things, what they are,
   that we may consider them,
or declare to us the things to come;
   that we may know their outcome.[9]
Tell us what is to come hereafter,
   that we may know that you are gods.

Finally this series of questions issues in the last almost despairing one:

Do good, or do harm [once and for all, for God's sake],
   that we may be dismayed and terrified

[that is, learn awe of the divine, the awe which takes hold of those of real insight]. Before such an attack the gods remain dumb. In the second series of comments Yahweh takes up the word of his own announcement of Cyrus, whom he has awakened and called by name, expressing it here in the question:

Who declared it from the beginning,
   that we might know,
and beforetime, that we might say,
   'He is right?'
There was none who declared it, none who proclaimed,
   none who heard your words.
I have first declared it to Zion,
   and I give to Jerusalem a herald of good tidings.

The 'I am the first and I am the last' of Isa. 44.6 is further developed in the same direction in vv. 7f.:

> Who is like me? Let him proclaim it,
>> let him declare and set it forth before me.
> Who has announced from of old the things to come?
>> Let them tell us what is yet to be.

And then the passage ends with the comforting sovereign approach of God to his people:

> Fear not, nor be afraid;
>> have I not told you from of old and declared it?
> And you are my witnesses!
> Is there a God besides me?
>> There is no Rock; I know not any.

(Cf. further also Isa. 45.21 and 46.9–11.)

It is against this background of Yahweh's absolute historical power toward the past and future that we should understand the overwhelming certainty mentioned earlier that God is capable of announcing something really new to the despairing people and of bringing this new thing to pass in a glory that far exceeds anything he has previously done. (Cf. Isa. 42.9; 43.18f.)

At one point in Isa. 48.3f. this reference to the prior proclamation of the 'new' is used polemically against Israel itself with the argument that the unbelief and stubbornness of the people will be overcome by means of this prophecy:

> The former things I declared of old,
>> they went forth from my mouth and I made them known;
>> then suddenly I did them and they came to pass.
> Because I know that you are obstinate,
>> and your neck is an iron sinew
>> and your forehead brass,
> I declared them to you from of old,
>> before they came to pass I announced them to you,
> lest you should say, 'My idol did them,
>> my graven image and my molten image commanded them.'

And a little further on (v. 7) the proclamation is again argued in the same way: 'lest you should say, "Behold, I knew them."' In these words another aspect appears which the prophet also opposes. In the suffering of the servant of God, in whose form and condition the office and condition of the prophet himself may find echo, and which God finally accepts as expiatory suffering for the guilt of the many, this new event finds its deepest substantiation and on its part becomes an event that is the basis of hope for the many.

This is not the place to develop further the message of Second Isaiah and to show how much he looked for a movement in the world of the nations which stood under the promissory oath of Yahweh:

> By myself I have sworn,
>   from my mouth has gone forth in righteousness
>   a word that shall not return:
> 'To me every knee shall bow,
>   every tongue shall swear.'
> Only in Yahweh, it shall be said of me,
>   are righteousness and strength . . . (Isa.45.23f.)

In this connection there emerges also that peculiar office of the prophet, described in the songs of the servant of God, in which he receives the assignment of becoming the light of the peoples (Isa. 49.6; cf.42.6).

In all this it has become clear how very much this prophet's message, over which stands the call in the introductory words, 'Comfort, comfort my people,' is a single great summons to lift up the head and step out hopefully into the promised future. Thus we hear at the outset in the prophet's own reflection on the people of God the assurance from his mouth:

> They who wait [hope, *qwh*] for Yahweh shall renew their
>   strength,
> they shall mount up with wings like eagles,
>   they shall run and not be weary,
> they shall walk and not faint. (Isa.40.31)

In 49.23 in the concluding formula of acknowledgment, a word of promise is put into the mouth of Yahweh:

> Then you will know that I am Yahweh;
> those who wait [hope *qwh*] for me shall not be put to shame.

The waiting that will not be put to shame extends however to the farthest coastlands which wait hopefully for the guidance of the servant of God (42.4 *yḥl*) and for the act of salvation by the strong arms of God (51.5 *qwh* ∥ *yḥl*).

But in all this it is surely clear that here also hope is not understood as a principle given in and with the world nor as an existential of human existence, but lives only in dependence upon the act of God announced in the word which goes out from him through his messenger. All the legitimacy of this hope rests solely in the pledge of the God who embraces history as the first and the last. Second Isaiah never wearies of glorifying his majesty and faithfulness.

A brief word may be said here about the later history of prophecy, which after the surprising and unique experience of a new beginning after the exile, which took as its historical starting point the edict of Cyrus calling for the rebuilding of the temple, then quickly ceased.

In the prophetic words of Isa. 56–66, which are summed up in oversimplified fashion with the catch-word 'Third Isaiah',[10] we recognize above all else the clear echo of the proclamation of Second Isaiah. In connection with our question about hope and a future it will suffice if we lift up a single powerful strain. Second Isaiah spoke his words to the exiles and opened before them the great hope for a return to Zion. The words of Third Isaiah, influenced by Second Isaiah, are spoken, as can be demonstrated in individual instances,[11] to those who again dwell in the land. One might assume that thus a large part of Second Isaiah's words would now fall away as fulfilled. In Isa. 57.14f. we hear the following summons, completely in the style of certain words of Second Isaiah:

> Build up, build up, prepare the way,
>   remove every obstruction from my people's way.
> For thus says the high and lofty One
>   who inhabits eternity, whose name is Holy:
> 'I dwell in the high and holy place,
>   and also with him who is of a contrite and humble spirit,
> to revive the spirit of the humble,
>   and to revive the heart of the contrite.'

The summons to build up the way, which must be understood literally in Second Isaiah, is here apparently taken over and understood as a command to remove all obstacles which might hinder the coming of God to his people. Similarly the whole word of comfort from the Most High to the lowliest is retained, even if now we are no longer faced with the real subjection of the exile. We hear this even more clearly in Isa. 61.1f., where the liberation of the captives is expressly mentioned. The phrases of Second Isaiah are here transcribed into a spiritual sense. The summons to look forward with hope is retained even in what are now changed circumstances. This can be most fully seen in ch. 60, a chapter that is full of echoes of Second Isaiah and before him of First Isaiah. In a powerful introduction Jerusalem is here summoned:

> Arise, shine; for your light has come,
>   and the glory of Yahweh has risen upon you.
> For behold, darkness shall cover the earth,
>   and thick darkness the peoples;
> but Yahweh will arise upon you,
>   and his glory will be seen upon you.

The subscription which concludes the broadly developed general passage about Zion, 'I am Yahweh; in its time I will hasten it,' enables us to recognize that this wakeful and hopeful expectation has its foundation in Yahweh alone, the living one through all time.

More clearly comprehensible are the two prophetic figures, Haggai and Zechariah,[12] to whose vigorous words are due the renewal of the previously half-hearted efforts to rebuild the Temple. We may recognize here the after-effects of the proclamation of Ezekiel and his school in that they firmly linked the coming of a new prosperity for the land to the pre-condition of the rebuilding of the Temple. Here and there one seems to hear in Zechariah an echo of the promises of Second Isaiah. On the other hand both Haggai and Zechariah are sharply distinguished from Second Isaiah in their message in that in them the old expectation of a Davidic king comes once more to full expression. In the governor appointed by the Persian king, Zerubbabel, who is of Davidic ancestry, both prophets see the ruler of the house of David promised by Yahweh in whom the promises shall be fulfilled. Zechariah speaks of him under the expression 'Branch', familiar from the proclamation of Jer. 23.5. In the unknown prophet who speaks in Jerusalem about the middle of the fifth century and whose words are found in the little book of Malachi, the expectation takes on different form as he anticipates the return of the prophet Elijah before the onset of the final day of judgment (Mal. 3.23).

But here, as in many statements of Zechariah, there appear new strains of thought. Granted one finds here also brief words in which Zechariah, in a manner similar to earlier prophets, announces a message of God directed primarily toward redemptive acts with a definite historical context. And one finds here also, again in the style of earlier prophets, a symbolic act which originally has for its setting the coronation of Zerubbabel as a messianic king (6.9–15).[13] Besides this, however, there is in about half of the book, filling up the eight chapters that derive from Zechariah himself, a sequence of eight, originally seven, night visions.[14] In these the direct statement recedes into the background. An interpreter here takes over the deciphering of the mysterious pictures that the prophet sees. In all this a new form of proclamation presents itself. In place of the prophet there emerges the writer of apocalyptic. With the examination of the apocalyptic parts of the Old Testament for their statement about hope and about a future in the biblical faith, we will conclude in the next chapter our journey through the Old Testament.

NOTES

[1] C. Westermann, *Isaiah 40–66* (OTL, 1969), pp. 3–292; G. Fohrer, *Das Buch Jesaja*, Bd. 3 (Zürcher Bibelkommentare, Zürich-Stuttgart 1964), pp. 1–183.

[2] W. Zimmerli, 'Der "neue Exodus" in der Verkündigung der beiden Exilspropheten', *Gottes Offenbarung* (ThB 19, 1963), pp. 192–204 (originally in French in *Maqqél shâqédh. La branche d'amandier. Hommage à Wilhelm Vischer* [Montpellier 1960], 216–227).

[3] J. Begrich, *Studien zu Deuterojesaja* (BWANT 4.25, 1938), pp. 6–19 (=ThB 20, 1963, pp. 14–26).

[4] G. von Rad, *Old Testament Theology* II, p. 247.

[5] Begrich, *op. cit.* (BWANT 4.25), pp. 112ff.

[6] Rearrangement and abbreviation according to Begrich, *ibid.*, pp. 45f. n. 3 (=ThB 20, p. 52 n. 180).

[7] W. Zimmerli, 'Der Wahrheitserweis Jahwes nach der Botschaft der beiden Exilspropheten, Tradition und Situation', *Studien zur alttestamentlichen Prophetie A. Weiser zum 70. Geburtstag dargebracht* (Göttingen 1963), pp. 133–51.

[8] Text emended at one point according to Begrich, *op. cit.*, pp. 40–42 (=47f.).

[9] The last two half-lines are inadvertently reversed in the Hebrew text.

[10] Westermann, *op. cit.*, pp. 295–429; Fohrer, *op. cit.*, pp. 184–285.

[11] W. Zimmerli, 'Zur Sprache Tritojesajas', *Festschrift für Ludwig Köhler* (Schweizerische theologische Umschau 20, 1950), pp. 110–22 (=*Gottes Offenbarung*, pp. 217–33).

[12] K. Elliger, *Kleinen Propheten* II (ATD 25⁵), pp. 83–143; Horst, *Kleinen Propheten* (HAT 14²), pp. 201–45.

[13] In the Hebrew text as we have it the high priest Joshua is substituted for Zerubbabel.

[14] 3.1–7, as the different formal shape of this night vision shows, has been added later.

X

THE HOPE OF FAITH ACCORDING TO
THE STATEMENTS OF APOCALYPTIC

WITH the Book of Daniel, the latest book of the Old Testament canon, a representative of apocalyptic thought joins the other writings of the Old Testament. In the same way the Revelation of John, also a document of this character, is taken up into the New Testament canon. One can document not only in these books which achieved canonical status, but also in a not unimpressive collection of non-canonical writings, especially from the inter-testamental, New Testament, and post-New Testament periods, two fundamental tendencies which are held together in tension in the apocalyptic writings.[1]

On the one hand there lives in the apocalyptic writings an eschatological impatience that stretches ever toward the end and the divine resolution of all the ambiguous things of this world through the last judgment.

This final event, at which as a rule all the power of the evil forces of earth are massed and anti-Christ figures take on meaning, is portrayed in all its sinister character.

To this eschatological impatience, however, there is repeatedly added a strikingly rational element, involving the desire to know and understand the world and its history. This can lead to representations of accurately worked out schemes of the sequence of historical events, in which the calculation of the various periods of history also plays an important role. Normally all this is not simply presented in direct address. Apocalyptic loves the veil of obscurity. Thus the description of events in the great apocalyptic writings is usually put in the mouth of a primeval figure empowered to predict the secret future. The particular revelation of information about the events of the last days is presented within the broad sweep of historical description in which, without concern for details, *vaticinium ex eventu*, the portrayal of what has already happened, is easily recognized. The event which is presented in a dream or vision, is concealed in pictures which are by no means directly understandable and which then require the *angelus interpres*, the heavenly interpreter figure who explains them. Thus a developed doctrine of angels makes its entrance in the apocalyptic writings. Of the interpretations it can be said more specifically that they are kept secret at first and thus initially represent the repetition of esoteric knowledge. The writer likes to present what he sees with suggestive vagueness. The seer sees 'something like . . .' In the figures used one can often recognize material that originates with earlier prophetic visions, material part of which is still available to us in the Old Testament scriptures. The apocalyptic writer has no intention of hiding this connection with earlier prophecy. His writing is presented frequently and quite openly as a new interpretation of an older word of God – as in Dan. 9, where the apocalyptic writer receives in a new revelation, involving a new way of calculating the numbers, the meaning of the seven years' famine in Jerusalem announced originally by Jeremiah. Thus apocalyptic writing can become scriptural exposition and the search for the mysterious second meaning hidden behind the open text of scripture.

To this attempt to give a brief general sketch of the outward form and appearance of apocalyptic discourse, we must add here a reference to certain basic elements:

1. The universality of its horizon. Here we are dealing as a rule not with certain areas of the world and their history but with the destiny of the world as a whole.
2. A definitely deterministic character. Here decisions are no longer open. The apocalyptic writer reveals the plan of God for the world, which is already determined and apparently can only run its course. In contrast to prophetic proclamation those responsible for the political future are no longer called to decision.
3. The tendency toward a dualistic view of total world events. A world headed toward the catastrophe of the great judgment stands over against the 'new' created by God. In the old aeon which is passing, the impending new aeon is proclaimed, a new aeon whose coming can no longer be affected by human decision because God has imparted to the apocalyptic writer his fixed decision.

The question of the origins of this characteristically apocalyptic form of statement has been the subject of lively discussion recently. In contrast to the view represented by most scholars that apocalyptic should be seen as a late form of prophecy, G. von Rad has defended doggedly the thesis that 'to understand apocalyptic literature as a child of prophecy is completely out of the question'.[2] His thesis points to the absence of any real contact with history, which according to the prophetic viewpoint is grounded for Israel in ancient foundations of salvation history. The apocalyptic writers, with their desire for knowledge, rather have their roots in the soil of wisdom literature, which reveals also this desire to know all things and the fundamental laws of their environment. But however correctly the undoubted difference between apocalyptic and prophecy is delineated, this thesis cannot be maintained in its extreme one-sidedness. One can without difficulty establish a counter-claim which reveals how very different apocalyptic literature is from wisdom literature with its consciousness of a coherent world of *maat*, of order,[3] the apocalyptic writings taking their shape from the impending rupture of time.

With all that clearly separates apocalyptic from prophecy, one must not overlook the fact that the former has its roots deep in the realm of prophetic proclamation of the radical judgment of God and the announcement of the new beginning beyond this judgment. It is not only that much of the imagery from prophetic visions has infiltrated the descriptions of the apocalyptic writers. In the structure of late prophecy itself, living no longer within a national body faced with political decisions, we see unmistakably the penetration of elements that could easily be identified as apocalyptic. This holds true, for example, of the announcement about Elijah in Mal. 4.5, in which Elijah is understood as the forerunner of the day of Yahweh itself. Here we have a description of a movement of final events occurring in phases. The relationship to prophetic writings is seen further in the place given to the interpreting angel in connection with the night visions of Zechariah (1.7ff.). And this interpreting angel has a definite predecessor in the man who, in the great final vision of the book of Ezekiel (40.3ff.), undertakes the measurement of the temple before the eyes of the seer. Thus however different prophecy and apocalyptic may be in their classical expressions, it is impossible to draw a clear-cut line of temporal separation between them.

So then at this point, before we speak about the book of Daniel, we will take another brief look at three complexes within the prophetic writings in which the impending approach of apocalyptic is increasingly foreshadowed.

First a word about Ezekiel 39f.[4] Here the prophet announces an invasion by an awful potentate, Gog, from the land of Magog, who leads the warring tribes of the mountain people from the north edge of the then known world. His attack is directed against the people who, again gathered from among the nations, live in peace upon the mountains of Israel. On these mountains Yahweh, at the end of the years, will destroy the enemy power concentrated here and invite the birds of the heavens and the beasts of the fields to the great sacrificial feast prepared by him – a powerful picture of the final victory of God over the enemy powers that assail his land.

In this proclamation of God there are unmistakable echoes not only of Jeremiah's announcement of the enemy from the north, but also of Isaiah's proclamation of the destruction of Assyria on the mountains of Palestine. There lives here the feeling that Jeremiah's proclamation is not completely satisfied by the intrusion of the Babylonians into Palestine, but rather that beyond the restoration of the 'House of Israel', which Ezekiel refers to as a new awakening, there waits yet a final threat to the people of God which Yahweh will bring to an end as in the predictions of Isaiah. In this projection beyond the deliverance of Israel to be immediately proclaimed, to one that will follow, an apocalyptic strain appears. The hope for a definite future for the life of God's people at the hand of their God is here divided between two acts of deliverance which are clearly distinguished from one another. Here is presented a programme of a definite future course of events filled with supernatural acts of God over which man has no influence.

We see clearly then in Ezek. 38f. that the event announced originally in a relatively simple text of three strophes has been expanded by means of additional supplementary material. This not only gives narrative colour to the whole, but also broadens it apocalyptically. Thus the judgment upon Gog is inserted into the framework of a cosmic shaking of the world. An earthquake will shake the whole world, even down to the fish in the sea. Mountains will crumble. Pouring rain and hail will fall. The portrayal of the burial of the legions of Gog undergoes an expansion to horrific proportions. It is no accident that the Gog prophecy subsequently

achieves a firm place, for example, in the Revelation (20.8f.) and
that the rabbinical traditions also speak continually of the 'Battle of
Gog and Magog'.

The book of Joel,[5] our second example here of the transition
from prophetic to apocalyptic statements of hope, speaks with
other tones. The occasion for his proclamation is, according to the
statements of ch. 1, a great plague of locusts which has swarmed
over the land. Earlier, in the visions of Amos (7.1–3), a locust
plague has appeared as the first harbinger of the far-reaching judgment of God. But in Joel the description of this affliction extends
to a description of the awful day of Yahweh. In Joel 2 the immediate distress caused by the locusts fades before the greater
danger of a strange and threatening enemy nation, in whom the
threat of the day of Yahweh emerges even more fully. In all this we
are still thoroughly within the realm of prophecy where, on the
basis of this word, the people are called to repentance and a
day of fasting in the temple is announced to the congregation. But
the whole picture takes on an apocalyptic colour when, after Yahweh's saving act is announced to the people, the story is expanded
into a world-wide event and a day of Yahweh involving the whole
of humanity is proclaimed. We are reminded here of Isaiah announcing salvation to those who dwell in Zion and who call upon
the name of Yahweh. But here we have a unique proclamation
which says that the Spirit of Yahweh will be poured out upon
the nation's sons and daughters, man-servants and maid-servants.
The day of judgment upon all peoples is announced by signs in
the heavens and on earth: blood and fire, the sun darkened and the
moon turned blood red. Then the nations, who in a reversal of the
expectation of peace in Isa. 2 are asked to beat their ploughshares
into swords and their pruning hooks into spears, are led by Yahweh into the valley of Jehoshaphat (the name means: Yahweh
judges). There Yahweh will execute a punitive judgment upon
them, a judgment that again takes place amid cosmic changes:

> The sun and the moon are darkened,
>   and the stars withdraw their shining.
> And the Lord roars from Zion,
>   and utters his voice from Jerusalem,
>   and the heavens and the earth shake.
> But the Lord is a refuge to his people,
>   a stronghold to the people of Israel. (Joel 3.15f.)

The land will become paradisally fruitful. The stream of water, known from Ezek. 47, will flow from the temple into the land and Israel's enemies will be destroyed. The prophetic element of a concrete historical call to repentance is unmistakable in the book of Joel. But at the same time the whole is interpenetrated by a cosmic outlook. The promise transcends all immediate partial situations and opens up views of a world-wide historical consummation. An older prophetic word is taken up and brought together in the vision of a final unique event.

> Has such a thing happened in your days,
>   or in the days of your fathers?

asks 1.2. And 2.2 says of the terrible invading peoples:

> Their like has never been from of old,
>   nor will be again after them
>   through the years of all generations.

Thirdly, we refer to the so-called Isaiah-Apocalypse in Isaiah 24–27,[6] a collection of eschatological sayings of anonymous tradition and late date, with songs accompanying the whole. The decisive statement of the entire collection, upon whose literary formation the last word has not yet been spoken, is found in chs. 24f. Here is described a terrible day of judgment which devastates the entire earth.

> The earth mourns and withers,
>   the world languishes and withers;
>   the heavens languish together with the earth.
> The earth lies polluted
>   under its inhabitants;
> for they have transgressed the laws,
>   violated the statutes,
>   broken the everlasting covenant. (Isa. 24.4f.)

The powers of the world 'the host of heaven, in heaven, and the kings of the earth' will be chained and called to account. We are reminded of Joel when in this connection we read:

> Then the moon will be confounded,
>   and the sun ashamed;
> for Yahweh of hosts will reign
>   on Mount Zion and in Jerusalem
> and before his elders he will manifest his glory. (Isa.24.23)

But beyond all there appears in Isa. 25.6–8 a view of the final redemption of the world which is described in the magnificent picture of the feast upon Mount Zion:

On this mountain Yahweh of hosts will make for all peoples a feast of
fat things, a feast of wine on the lees, of fat things full of marrow, of
wine on the lees well refined. And he will destroy on this mountain the
covering that is cast over all peoples, the veil that is spread over all
nations. He will swallow up death for ever,[7] and Yahweh will wipe
away tears from all faces, and the reproach of his people he will take
away from all the earth; for Yahweh has spoken.

Granted that all elements of speculation about the times, or
mysterious comparisons in images that need interpretation, or recognizable temporal-historical relationships, are absent here. But
very clearly evident is the element of a great breakthrough beyond
the final affliction of judgment that will come upon the world, a
breakthrough in a surprising openness of expectation to a word of
salvation which the peoples of the world apparently will share.
The double relationship of these statements to both prophecy and
apocalyptic writing is also difficult to overlook.

Now it is in order to turn to the book of Daniel.[8] As even a
cursory glance reveals, this book falls into two very different sections. After the introduction of Daniel and his three friends who,
according to the testimony of the book itself, have been taken by
Nebuchadnezzar to Babylon as exiles, the first six chapters relate
five fairly self-contained legends about the trials and preservation
of these men in the heathen court. Chapter 2, which reports
Daniel's interpretation of the dream of Nebuchadnezzar, and ch. 5,
which describes his deciphering of the puzzling inscription on the
wall at Belshazzar's feast, creates content-wise the bridge to the
second half of the book which presents apocalyptic revelations exclusively. Recent research has made it certain that the book in its
present form originates from the time of the religious persecutions
of the Seleucid king, Antiochus IV Epiphanes. More precisely we
can say that it was compiled between 167 and 163. But on the other
hand it is equally clear that, in the little book of legends and possibly also in ch. 7, older material that goes back to the third century is
used. But we cannot pursue further here these literary and historical
questions, as for example the striking fact that from 2.4b to 7.28 the
book of Daniel is written in Aramaic whereas the rest is in Hebrew.[9]

The apocalyptic sections, which must chiefly concern us in connection with our general question about hope in the Old Testament, differ in details. The dream of Nebuchadnezzar in ch. 2, as
also the dream and vision of Daniel in chs. 7 and 8, are concealed
in pictorial language. According to ch. 2 Nebuchadnezzar sees a
great image made of various metals that is shattered by a stone
thrown by an invisible hand. Daniel is not only able to tell the
dream to the king, who mistrusts all his own sorcerers, who are
unable to reveal its contents, but is able to interpret its meaning.
In Daniel's dream in ch. 7 there are four animals that rise out of the
sea, a lion with eagle's wings, a bear, a leopard, and a dreadful
fourth animal with ten horns. Upon this last animal a heavenly
court sits in judgment and all power is given over to one (a son of
man) who comes on the clouds of heaven. Daniel in this puzzling
vision indicates that this is a divine figure. In the vision in ch. 8
animals also appear to Daniel: a ram and a he-goat with one, then
four, and then yet a fifth horn, which desecrates the sanctuary.
Here it is the heavenly figure of Gabriel who interprets the picture
for Daniel and announces a time of trouble and its end as intended
by the vision. This valid pictorial language is given up in ch. 9,
where Daniel reflects upon the seventy years of trouble announced
by Jeremiah (25.11f.; 29.10) and, in the course of a despairing
prayer of repentance, learns from Gabriel the interpretation of the
years as weeks of years, and is told that the greatest time of trouble
will come with the last week and will then end. In the great final
revelation of chs. 10–12 a divine figure who is introduced in great
detail finally describes at first hand the war between the kings of
the north and the south, that is, the Ptolemies and the Seleucids,
their sudden end in the immeasurable infamy of the last king of the
north, and then his death 'between the sea and the glorious holy
mountain'. Through final troubles there then occurs the deliverance
of the people of God, the resurrection of the righteous to salvation
and the godless to torment.

Wherein lies the peculiar character of the announcement of the
future expressed in the various formulations of apocalyptic speech?
It is first of all clear that, in the statements of the book of Daniel,
what dominates is not the element of gnosis but rather the glowing
expectation of the imminent end which announces itself amid the
oppression of the time of trouble. Out of the oppression created
by the desecration of the sanctuary through the establishment of

the 'desolation of abominations', that is the image of Zeus, the 'heavenly Baal' in the temple, expectation of the imminent end arises. It should be recognized that the calculation of the intervening times is bound up with this hopeful waiting. Two thousand and three hundred evenings and mornings, that is 1150 days, is the time according to 8.14 of the desecration of the sanctuary, which according to 9.27 corresponds to the second half of the seventieth week of years. In 12.11 this end date is easily postponed: '. . . from the time that the continual burnt offering is taken away and the abomination that makes desolate is set up, there shall be a thousand two hundred and ninety days.' This appears to lead to a time span of three and a half years and an intercalary month. 12.12, which is apparently a later addition, has on the other hand this formulation: 'Blessed is he who waits (*ḥkh*) and comes to the thousand three hundred and thirty-five days.' Here there is encouragement to hope, even with the appropriate vocabulary. The hot breath of one who scarcely is able to endure against the desolation breathes upon us in these calculations. The waiting in 9.27 looks toward that point in time in which 'upon the wing of abominations shall come one who makes desolate, until the decreed end is poured out on the desolator.' The formula is taken over from Isaiah (10.23; 28.22). 11.45 puts it directly: the oppressor 'shall come to his end, with none to help him'. '. . . by no human hand, he shall be broken' (8.25). But this simple reference to the end of the oppression by no means completely represents the full dimension of the expectation. If in ch. 9 we can see that this end is at the same time the end of the 70 long weeks of years of trouble and therefore the conclusion of an epoch of even longer duration, then according to the view of ch. 8, the end of the war between the powers represented by the ram and he-goat has also been reached. As in antique astral geography, Persia has the animal sign of the ram and Syria that of the he-goat, the thought here may be of a conflict between these powers, that is between Persia and the Greek world as it was represented from the viewpoint of Palestine by the Syrian Seleucids. In ch. 11, moreover, there is, in a long excursus, a historical account that goes back as far as the Persian period. This history is recapitulated quite accurately to the time of Antiochus IV. Where the description no longer coincides with real history, it is clear that we have the onset of the peculiarly apocalyptic predictions.

But this return to the previous history of Persia does make completely clear the dimension in which the expected end of the oppressor stands. The full breadth of the statement is first recognizable in the descriptions of chs. 2 and 7. Here the scheme of the four periods of world history is used in a variety of ways to represent the earlier history which ends in the overthrow of the oppressor. In ch. 2 this is done in a very striking manner by means of a picture of a monumental statue, whose head is made of gold, breast of silver, belly and thighs of bronze, and legs and feet of iron. (The addition of clay to the feet we owe to a later expansion.) The interpretation points to the succession of Babylonian, Median, Persian, and Greek empires. This scheme of a succession of world-empires, originating in Media, and from this perspective involving Assyria, Media, Persia, and Greece, is also found in Roman sources. Its quadruple character refers not just to an arbitrarily chosen partial listing, but to the totality of all great empires. In the four empires of ch. 2 is embraced the totality of the history of great empires.[10]

But in the reference to the metals of descending value, there is bound up a second line of thought. This is evident also in Hesiod's idea of periods of world history; he introduces the metals as identifying marks of these. In Daniel these periods are not distinguished by political systems; the thought is of descending value. Through four periods the world is on the way to depravation and is ever more ripe for judgment. In the sudden judgment upon the last representative of the fourth period, this process is consummated.

This background is much more clearly evident in the quite different movement of the picture in ch. 7. Four animals of ever less nobility, but ever greater ferocity arise out of the sea, the ancient sphere of the power of chaos. But at the end of the periods of world-powers as represented by the animals, there stands the heavenly judgment in which the (son of) man who descends upon the clouds of heaven is given power and glory and a kingdom. Here the collapse of the old world of historical powers as a historical entity, the world that arises from below, from the powers of the chaos, pictured here by ever more hideous animal figures, is given unmistakable expression.

The new thing which takes the place of the old is described in ch. 2, with an attempt at imagery, as the stone cut without human hand, a stone which becomes a huge mountain and fills the whole earth. With the stone the thought of solidity and dependability is given expression. The interpretation makes this clear, with the words:

The God of heaven will set up a kingdom which shall never be destroyed, nor shall its sovereignty be left to another people. It shall break in pieces all these kingdoms and bring them to an end. (2.44)

In ch. 7 the new is represented in more expressive and pictorial language as the figure of a man who descends from above:

And to him was given dominion and glory and kingdom, that all peoples, nations, and languages should serve him; his dominion is an everlasting dominion, which shall not pass away, and his kingdom one that shall not be destroyed. (7.14)

But the interpretation then says:

And the kingdom and the dominion and the greatness of the kingdoms under the whole heaven shall be given to the people of the saints of the Most High; their kingdom shall be an everlasting kingdom, and all dominions shall serve and obey them. (7.27)

Here the transitory world of the powers subject to judgment is very clearly contrasted with the new world of God's people, an old aeon that is passing over against a new one that is to come. How completely unprecedented this 'new' theory, made new by the power of divine creative glory, will be, is made clear in the concluding statements of the final great revelation. This speaks of the final deliverance of the people of God: 'At that time your people shall be delivered, every one whose name shall be found in the book [of life] (12.1).' But with this there is linked the event of resurrection, which breaks open the world of death. The passage continues:

And many of those who sleep in the dust of the earth shall awake, some to everlasting life, and some to shame and everlasting contempt. And those who are wise shall shine like the brightness of the firmament; and those who turn many to righteousness, like the stars for ever and ever. (12.2f.)

If we ask on what grounds the faith of the apocalyptic writer dares to hope so determinedly for the change of aeons which will bring the people of God freedom and redemption, the answer must be that no basis in salvation history is indicated in these chapters. Thoughts in this direction are found solely in the long prayer of Daniel in ch. 9, a prayer whose relationship to its context there is questionable. But the knowledge of God's faithfulness to his people is never discussed at all. It is a certainty explicated no further that is simply assumed as a background to all that is said. Only in the final revelation can we see the curtain lifted for a brief moment as 10.21 and 12.1 tell how Michael, the great prince, intervenes for the people of God in the angel-world and there foreshadows the struggle of the political powers. Among the multitude of transcendent powers, so this word may perhaps be expressed, the God of heaven had destined the mightiest, Michael, the great prince, to be the helper of Israel.

In all that we have pursued thus far, it is 'hope' in its objective form – as the look toward the future expected from God – that has come into plain view.

But in conclusion one question presents itself: within such an expectation, what does man's personal hope appear to be? In the midst of oppressive misery and in view of the emphatic statement about the impending divine future for those who hope, who know that God has determined the course of things and no man can stop the wheels of this process, is there anything else to do other than to wait with hands folded in one's lap? The apocalyptic writer does not leave us without an answer here. He knows that in fact an expectant looking ('the endurance and faith of the saints' is the way Rev. 13.10 formulates it) is the mark of the human stance shaped by his proclamation. But this looking forward is not an apathetic waiting and empty killing of time. Rather this waiting focuses the eye directly toward the God who promises the future, and seeks at the same time in the restricted freedom of individual decisions, even when these are no longer able to shape history, to be patiently obedient toward God and to exalt his honour.

Thus the legends of Dan. 1–6 do not just happen to be the basis for the apocalyptic expansion of the book of Daniel. However obvious it may be that they did not originate at the time of great hostility and tension under the foreign ruler Antiochus IV, but presuppose throughout a much quieter relationship to heathen authority, nevertheless these stories of the faithfulness of Daniel and his three friends take their meaning directly from this new setting. For patient faith cannot speak otherwise, even in the time of Maccabean persecution, than did the three men who, when confronted with the threat of the fiery furnace, still refused to worship the image that Nebuchadnezzar had erected.

If it be so [that we be thrown into the fiery furnace], our God whom we
serve is able to deliver us from the burning fiery furnace; and he will
deliver us out of your hand, O king. But if not, be it known to you, O
king, that we will not serve your gods or worship the golden image
which you have set up. (3.17f.)

Here both words are uttered side by side, in almost unbearable
tension: God can save those who belong to him from the fire and
he will also do it. But at the same time he is the one who is free,
who has the power to manage things according to his mysterious
wisdom. But human obedience remains, even in the light of this
freedom, obedience toward God. Here too, on a completely different level, the thought of the wise friends of Job, which has God
encapsulated in a world of calculable order, is rejected. Hope hopes
in God, the God whose freedom men do not take away by hoping,
no matter how immovably certain they are of the promise of
God to his own, no matter how they cling to that promise. It is
upon this foundation that the hope of the apocalyptic writer rests.

NOTES

[1] Cf. e.g. H. H. Rowley, *The Relevance of Apocalyptic: a Study of Jewish and
Christian Apocalypses from Daniel to the Revelation* (London 1944; 2nd ed.
revised, New York 1946); also O. Ploeger, *Theokratie und Eschatologie*
(WMANT 2, 1959).

[2] G. von Rad, *Old Testament Theology* II, p.303.

[3] See above, p.15

[4] On this point cf. the commentaries listed in ch. VIII, n.8, p.121 above.

[5] Weiser, *Kleinen Propheten* (ATD 24⁴), pp.105-27; Robinson, *Kleinen Propheten* (HAT 14²), pp.55-69; H. W. Wolff, *Dodekapropheton* II (BKAT 14.2),
pp.1-104. Also Ploeger, *op. cit.*, pp.117-28.

[6] Cf. the commentaries referred to in ch. VII, n.11, p.105 above; also
Ploeger, op. cit., pp.69-97.

[7] Whether this section of this sentence is original is a matter of dispute.

[8] N. W. Porteous, *Daniel* (OTL, 1965); A. Bentzen, *Daniel* (HAT 19²,
1952); O. Ploeger, *Das Buch Daniel* (KAT 18, 1965); also Ploeger, *Theokratie
und Eschatologie*, pp.19-36.

[9] Cf. on this the commentaries mentioned in the previous note.

[10] Cf. in this connection what is said on p.59 above about the priestly
writings.

XI

CONVERSATION WITH ERNST BLOCH

THE question about man's hope which has accompanied us on our journey through the various sections of the Old Testament, has been raised in our time in especially impressive fashion by Ernst Bloch in his great work entitled *Das Prinzip Hoffnung*.[1] He calls to a time shaped by fear: 'Everything comes down to this, that we learn to hope.'[2] This is a matter of learning to distinguish between false and authentic hope:

Corruptio optimi pessima: fraudulent hope is one of the greatest malefactors, enervating the generations of man, but concrete authentic hope one of his most genuine benefactors.[3]

In this Bloch does not intend to present something that is entirely new, that has never penetrated the human spirit before.

The good thing that is new is never so very new. Its impact goes far beyond the day-dreams that penetrate all of life and fill the creative arts. Utopian desires guide all movements for freedom and all Christians also recognize this in their fashion, whether with sleeping conscience or with amazement, in the story of the Exodus and in the messianic passages of the Bible.[4]

Here the reader of the Bible is challenged, asked about his understanding of the Bible. We will concern ourselves in this last chapter with the conversation that Bloch's words demand, the conversation about the words of the Bible to which Ernst Bloch appeals as a witness for his presentation of the Principle of Hope. In these last moments of reflection we will clearly limit ourselves to conversation about the sphere of the Old Testament outlined. In his appeal to the Exodus and messianic passages of the Bible, Bloch has in a special way reclaimed the Old Testament, where these two themes originate, for the 'Principle of Hope'.

Everything that follows presupposes the summary in which Bloch at the conclusion of his book describes how he, following Karl Marx, believes he must see 'the Development of the Wealth of Human Nature', to which the principle of hope fundamentally belongs.

This *human* wealth, like that of nature in general, lies solely in the latent tendency in which the world finds itself – before everything. This view also holds that man still lives everywhere in pre-history, yes, each and everything stands yet before the creation of the world as a true world. *The real Genesis is not at the beginning but at the end,* and it begins first when society and existence first become radical, that is, take hold of themselves at their very roots. But the roots of history lie in the working, creating man who transforms and surpasses what is given. If he has taken hold of himself and established that which is his in real democracy without renunciation or alienation, then there arises in the world something which everyone saw in childhood but no one ever really inhabited: home.[5]

The central key-word from which Bloch believes one must understand the Old Testament is, as one would assume from one of the initial quotations, the word 'Exodus'. Alongside of the event of the Exodus there stands Moses, law-giver and first leader into freedom.

What does Scripture relate immediately after it becomes historical? It tells of the suffering of an enslaved people that must carry bricks, work as slaves in the field, and 'there life became bitter for them'. Moses appears, strikes down a taskmaster – it is the first act of the future founder of the nation – and he is forced to leave the land. The God whom he imagines in a strange land is right at the outset not a God who lords it over his worshippers, but a free Beduin of the Sinai area of Kenitic nomadic tribes into which Moses has married. Yahweh begins as a threat to Pharaoh, the volcanic God of Sinai becomes with Moses the God of liberation, escape from servitude. In this fashion Exodus gives the Bible right from this point its fundamental tone, which it has never lost.[6]

In connection with this determination of origins Bloch establishes on the one hand that 'remembrance of nomadic structures exhibiting features of primitive communism' are in no book 'so strongly retained as in the Bible'.[7] This remembrance comes to life again and again after the people have arrived in the land of Canaan, where private property comes into being. Hosea's and Jeremiah's proclamation contain reminiscences of the wilderness period as the good time of the honeymoon. On the other hand it is important for Bloch that with the Exodus not only the category of 'front' is opened up in which the newness of movement in 'militant optimism' interrupts the static desire to wait, but that even here the conception of newness, which admittedly appears elsewhere also, is established.

The new . . . runs through the expectation of almost all religions, in so far as the primitive and also the old oriental consciousness of the future can be correctly understood. It penetrates the entire Bible from Jacob's blessing to the Son of man who makes all things new and the new heaven and new earth.[8]

If religion in general involves the sense of encounter with the strange ('this remoteness, yes even this dread of the brink belongs to every religious relationship, or it is not one'),[9] then the act of leading out and the consequent giving of the law bring fully into play the revolutionary leap into the wholly new.

With Moses there occurred a leap in religious consciousness, and this was prepared through an event which stands in the greatest possible opposition to all previous religions, religions of this-worldly piety or of astral mythical destiny; prepared through rebellion, through the Exodus from Egypt. In this way, in contrast to such figures as Nimrod or a great self-exalting medicine man, did Moses become the first eponymous hero, the first originator by name of a religion of opposition. Other later religions of opposition such as the warlike Zoroastrianism, the a-cosmic Buddhism, are understandable to Europeans only on the basis of the Exodus archetype.[10]

For Bloch then the key-word 'Exodus' contains a double meaning. Of the Christian faith he says at one point:

[Thus] the wonder-being, Christ, beyond his temporary world-view, is in accord at two main points with that which is conceivable today: formally in the matter of discontinuity, materially with respect to absolutely good content.[11]

The category of discontinuity is maintained also by the miracle:

However much the essence of miracle descended [in medieval times] into banal occultism, . . . the conception of the miraculous, apart from its transcendent superstition, did significantly contain the

thoroughly unsuperstitious conception of discontinuity which origi-
nated with a faith in discontinuity. It is precisely from the notion of the
miraculous that the conception of discontinuity is learned.[12]

Therefore, on the one hand the Exodus led by Moses is the first
phenomenon of discontinuity which shapes all that follows. At
the same time one finds in the act of Moses the 'material of the
absolutely good content'.

An enslaved people – this is the point of distress that teaches one to
pray. And a founder appears who begins by striking down a taskmaster.
Thus suffering and indignation stand together at the beginning, and
make of faith at the outset a way into freedom. The God of Sinai,
taken over from the Kenites, does not remain with Moses the local god
of a volcano, but becomes the spirit of Exodus.[13]

But now this spirit of the Exodus is recognizable in the contents
of the decalogue.

Even as the Exodus is Mosaic and not Kenite, so there is preserved in
the matrix of the decalogue a creation of Moses, not a moral code of the
Canaanites nor yet, from even farther away, one taken over from the
ancient Babylonian monarch Hammurabi. His book of law from 2100[14]
has about as much in common with the decalogue as the *corpus juris*
with the Kantian moral imperative . . . the unbroken communal ethic
that Moses formulated did not exist in Canaan.[15]

This holds true even when we realize that many things do not become clear until subsequent periods of time.

A sentence such as 'You shall love your neighbour as yourself' (Lev.
19.18), as a concentration of the ten commandments in one, had its first
unconscious beginnings in the primitive community: the bringing to
consciousness and almost harsh enactment is the work of Moses. As
this it was also kept in remembrance by Israel.[16]

We must be careful not to misunderstand what Bloch is saying
here. He is not saying that Moses, by means of a revolutionary act,
has again brought into force that element of 'communal ethic', the
'primitive community' that was already in an earlier epoch an element of tribal life in the Beduin area, it now being a matter of
action after the fact to create new validity for this old inheritance.
The 'discontinuity' in the act of Moses leads into something which
is truly new, but which for its part is not therefore absolutized and

made into a final goal. Rather in the 'Exodus' it is the ever renewed openness for the new that is especially manifested.

Through the intervention of Moses the content of salvation is changed from that which the heathen religions, especially the astral and mythical, had set as their fully established external goal. In place of the established goal there now appears a goal that is promised but that first must be won; in place of the visible god of nature there appears an invisible one of righteousness and the kingdom of righteousness.[17]

The meaning of the Exodus consists in the fact that here hope is opened up toward the future which man goes to meet. 'Canaan' is the key-word for this future, towards which Israel, and mankind in Israel, goes forward.

This existence in which man is called into a future that is always disclosing itself anew, and which then later is most adequately summed up in the word 'kingdom', Bloch sees expressed also in the revelation of the name of God, as it is imparted to Moses according to Ex. 3.14. When Yahweh here in response to the question about his name, introduces himself to Moses as *'ehyeh 'ašer 'ehyeh*, which Bloch translates as 'I will be what I will be', he makes known the absolute distinction between him and all the other gods, including according to Bloch the god of the rabbinical law fixed about 450 BC, as well as the lordly god whom the Israelites really took over with the land and worshipped as Baal. Here God expresses his own special being. This definition of this name 'derives from no priestly codex, but from the original spirit of the Exodus itself'.[18] Whatever might be said about the time when the declaration of the name was made, the intention is 'here autochthonous, that is, delineation of a real intention, the same one that moves the local god of Sinai toward the future Canaan as his far-off homeland'.[19] *'ehyeh 'ašer 'ehyeh* 'presents, at the very threshold of the appearance of Yahweh, a God of the end of days, with futurity as the characteristic of his being'.[20] Thus Bloch on the basis of this name can speak of the *Deus Spes*, that is, the God whose essence is hope.

It is from this aspect that we are to understand everything else that Bloch brings into prominence in the Old Testament. This is his point of departure as he speaks of 'the half-nomadic Nazirite opposition . . . very near to the Beduins . . . rude figures withdrawn from civilization', or the 'Rechabites, a tribe in the

south who remain at a distance from the luxury and money
economy of Canaan and remain faithful to the old wilderness
God'.[21] In these opponents, rebels against the faith of the people
dwelling in the land, we hear, according to Bloch, not a return to
the ancient past, a conservative clinging to a past social and cultural order – not even if that were the good old Beduin communism – but rather a breaking out, a turn to the new, opposition
to inhumanity, opposition to an evil social structure out of which
one desires to break into a newer better life. This is clear in the
prophets. In them there burns the brightest protest against the
'turning from the (as it were) pre-capitalistic Yahweh to Baal, and
also to the lordly Yahweh, who had defeated Baal at the price of
himself becoming a God of luxury'.[22]

Amos, who says of himself that he is a poor shepherd who picks mul-
berries, is the earliest of the prophets . . . perhaps the greatest: and his
Yahweh lights the match. 'I will send a fire upon Judah, and it shall
devour the strongholds of Jerusalem . . . because they sell the righteous for silver, and the needy for a pair of shoes – they that trample
the head of the poor into the dust of the earth, and turn aside the way
of the afflicted' (Amos 2.5–7).[23]

Here it is very clear that his proclamation is not directed to a
return to the past, but rather expresses an attitude of expectation.
'The day is certain in which the spirit of liberation, Yahweh, the
God of the Exodus, will be alive again.'[24] Thus that day is now
awaited in which the law will go out from Zion and swords will be
turned into ploughshares.

The content of the biblically intended future has remained discernible
in all social utopias: Israel became the poor, Zion the utopia. Tribulation makes one messianic.[25]

Thus there followed from this the messianic expectation that is
taken up more fully in the New Testament with the appearance of
Jesus. Here the expectation of the kingdom begins to come alive –
a kingdom not to be misinterpreted as a spiritualized beyond, but
to be understood as an event 'upon this present visible stage'.[26]
    This concluding world-wide perspective of hope is not alien to
the beginnings of the faith of Israel:

With Moses . . . the *Deus Spes* is already sketched, even if the picture
of the final deliverer from Egypt, in other words, the Messiah, does not

appear until a thousand years later; messianism is older than this messianic faith.[27]

In this expansion of hope to include the whole world the intention of the prophet achieves its proper development. In open polemic against Moses Hess and the newer Zionism, Bloch formulates it thus:

According to the intention of the prophets, Zion is everywhere and the local mountain in Palestine has long ago become a symbol . . . Zionism is expressed in Socialism, or it is not expressed at all.[28]

It is within this framework then that we should view the expectation of the paradise to be regained on earth. If the land of Canaan is the initial goal of paradise expectations for those who came through the Exodus, then the messianic dimension is later added:

Not until the end of history does Canaan appear complete, with Mount Zion in its midst; . . . at the end of days the earthly paradise is again open. It appears again and may be entered, in that the heavenly Jerusalem comes to earth (Rev. 21.2), but not until the end of time.[29]

This *Deus Spes,* who causes man to step out into the future in hope, has essentially one great enemy: the Creator God who has created a good world in the beginning. According to Bloch, Gen. 1, the chapter that speaks of the creation of the world with ever repeated reference to the fact that what God created was good, embodies the proclamation fundamentally antithetical to the *Deus Spes.* The master-builder god Ptah of Egypt and the Babylonian imperial god Marduk are for Bloch the godfathers of the priestly account of Gen. 1.

The Babylonian imperial god Marduk, as the founder of order, is united with Ptah, the founder of the world, the supreme cosmic ruler with the supreme cosmic founder, everything from the beginning of the world already flawlessly complete, with the division of the waters of heaven and earth, with the forming of the earth. Now the account of the beginning of the world, and even its alleged perfection, are first introduced into the Bible, appearing to require no further home beyond, no Exodus from the present . . . But this perfection is referred to only on one occasion in the Bible (Gen. 1.31) . . . That the world is a work of art itself, completed by the highest God, originates in the land of opposition to the Bible: in Egypt and Babylon. For Yahweh, as the God of the Exodus from Egypt, already stands in opposition to the present world as a standard of measure; his Canaan is not the cosmos. The God of Isaiah is downright unfriendly, not to say rebellious against a finished cosmos and, above all, against the one that has become so here on earth for the Jews. He rather promises a new heaven and a new earth, so that men will no longer remember the former one, that is the Genesis one (Isa. 65.17). And only for this homeland on the other side, for Canaan which requires the Exodus for its realization, was a non-heathen architecture, anti-Egyptian *par excellence,* appropriate.[30]

Yet there is absent from the picture of biblical speech about the *Deus Spes,* as Bloch sketches it, an essential strain. Bloch entitles ch. 53 of his *Prinzip Hoffnung* 'The Awakening Human Insight Into The Religious Secrets of Astral-mythology, Exodus, Kingdom; Atheism and the Utopia of the Kingdom'.[31] In listening to the statements of religion and especially the biblical word, Bloch believes he can identify the increasing intrusion of the human founder himself into the message proclaimed by him.

The founders of faith intrude themselves increasingly into their 'wholly other', making it more and more into a human mystery or a mystery with content mediated by humans. The power of this unrestrained inclusion, the call of this pious penetration works out to this: 'I will not let you go unless you bless me.' (Gen. 32.26)[32]

His words make clear that Bloch is not thinking here of a cultural secularization in which the mystery of the numinous is finally and decisively done away with in an atheism that gives place to the intellect alone. Even when he says, 'How often has man recognized in this intrusion that he is better than his gods',[33] he is making reference to the fact that with such surpassal of the gods 'the foundation of a new mystery'[34] arose.

Numen, numinous, mysterium, absolute no to the given world, are nothing other than mysterious humanity itself: properly understood, the mystery, that which hides itself, that through which the discontinuity of the wholly other is completely different from the known and immanently filled environment.[35]

If in the race toward the goal of hope, faith in God is lost along the way, it remains true that 'the kingdom . . . is the central religious conception'.[36] This 'totality of hope' has room for the swift movement toward fulfilled humanity. 'Aiming for a religious kingdom in itself at the end of the day involves atheism.'[37] At the end of this road stands not the *mysterium* of the *deus absconditus,* but that of the *homo absconditus.* But this not in a spiritualized sense as the enemy of the earth, but in the immediate revolutionary turn toward a new order of humanity in a classless and truly human society. Thus Bloch, on the basis of this point of view, can set himself bluntly against the Zionism that looks toward Jerusalem. 'Ubi Lenin, ibi Jerusalem.'[38] In the realism of this concern with the human figures of the world, one can understand the sentence: 'Without atheism there is no room for messianism.'[39]

Such intrusion of the human into the religious Bloch sees arising in the biblical sphere.

The Dionysian founder vanishes before his god of nature, the astral mythical founder fades before him, and even Buddha, the self-saviour, is engulfed at the end in an a-cosmic Nirvana . . . Moses on the other hand forces God to go with him, makes him an Exodus light to a people. Jesus presses beyond the transcendent as a human tribunal, and utopianizes it as the kingdom.[40]

In Moses' saving leadership of his people what happens to the local god of Sinai is:

The local god is taken from his setting and through his vicegerent, Moses, becomes cloud and pillar of fire, moves out with a people originally strange to him into the unknown.[41]

So powerfully 'was the content of salvation changed by the intervention of Moses'.[42] This can be seen in the prophets also. Because in contrast to Cassandra, who proclaims an empty fate, they know of the God 'I will be whom I will be', they find themselves thrown into the place of freedom created therein:

Destiny can be completely changed; Isaiah in particular teaches it as dependent upon man's morality and his decisions.[43] . . . With this intervention by morality into the shape of destiny a counter-movement of freedom is opened up. . . . This is directed outwardly against fate, in concealed manner against its Lord, who is repeatedly called to justice.[44]

But Bloch believes that he finds this faith most powerfully expressed in the Old Testament in the rebellion of Job, the Hebrew Prometheus. Here the exodus becomes radical.

Has not . . . the book of Job . . . brought something completely unique to add to the faith of Moses, that is, the rejection of that faith? As rejection of his joyful message, as indignation–and now not only against Pharaoh or Baal and Belial, but against the Yahweh of a fictitious

justice himself . . . Neither the lame correctness and traditional har-
monies of his friends nor the thunderstorm in which Yahweh makes
known his unique grandeur, salvages faith in the justice of the God
once so grandly proclaimed and proclaiming himself. Before a mind
that will no longer submit, the theocracy that has become inhuman can
no longer stand.[45]

But what appears at first as a contradiction of all other statements of
the Old Testament, is 'authentic Old Testament, or Moses in a
Contra-Moses'.[46] For here the exodus reality achieves its sharpest
form. At the same time it becomes clear (if we may formulate it as
elsewhere), that the *Deus Spes* is actually *not* a *Deus Spes*, but is over-
powered by the humanity that is the final content of hope. The
Deus (God) disappears, where *Spes* (hope) in its ultimate intention
becomes reality.

For Job the exodus becomes radical: not simply as a measurement of
Yahweh against the ideal of his justice and the kingdom of justice, but
as an exodus from Yahweh himself into the unknown Canaan of which
he was the unfulfilled promise. 'I know that my vindicator lives, and at
last he will stand over my dust. The witness to my innocence will be
with me and my deliverer from guilt I will see for myself, with my own
eyes and with no other' (Job 19.25–27). The messianic faith of this text,
corrupted to be sure and not without reason, thus leaves Yahweh behind – for the sake of his utopia.[47]

But this way of exodus from Yahweh, which includes in its
course the Preacher of Ecclesiastes,[48] is completed in the institution
of Christ, who introduces himself in his message as the 'son of
man' and who carries out the complete identification of the institution with the content of the institution.

The joyful message operates theologically as the suspension of the
absolute divine transcendence through the homousia, the divinity of
Christ. It operates democratically and mystically as the fulfilment of the
God of the Exodus in the kingdom, in the dissolution of Yahweh in
this glory.[49]

In this connection Bloch can also introduce the teaching of the
Naassenes or Ophites, according to which the serpent of paradise
is understood as a being both subversive and redemptive. This
serpent, who leads man to a knowledge of good and evil and who
is identified with the healing serpent set up by Moses in the wilderness (Num. 21.9), which according to John 3.14 is a picture of the

uplifted Christ, again makes clear the contradiction between the saviour and the Creator-Yahweh.[50]

Bloch's violent and impetuous expropriation of the Old Testament calls for discussion of this book. Is this expropriation justified?

In the first place it is impossible to overlook the fact that Bloch has indeed impressively demonstrated the strongly hopeful character of Old Testament statements which not only look backward but repeatedly betray a surprising openness toward the future. The essential question that must be asked here, however, suppressing at this point all detailed observations that might be made with respect to particularities of exegetical treatment, is this: Does Ernst Bloch, in his broadly sketched interpretation of the general phenomenon of hope, do justice to the deepest concerns that shape the Old Testament statements about hope?

Our look through the Old Testament statements considered in the previous chapters led repeatedly and with surprising persistence to one central point from which all statements about hope proceeded. It became clear that it was precisely where man was led to the edge of human hopelessness that every look turned away from man and his immanent possibilities. There was at no place a 'principle of hope' that was generally held or believed by man, no existential hope to be discovered in the existential understanding of man or in his understanding of his world. Rather it became clear that it was precisely where the sharpest criticisms of hope were loudest, that man in a frightening recklessness threw himself upon the one he was conscious of as coming to his people, or in the broadest meaning, to his creation. At this point one should especially name that book which Bloch introduces as his prize witness for his 'exodus from Yahweh himself', the book of Job. In all the passion of Job's dealings with the comforting theology of his friends, which appointed God his admittedly not unimportant place in their teleological thought-frame, what fed the fire of his passion was at no point exodus from God, but rather far more a zeal for God, the living and mysterious, who could not be so easily harnessed to a clever theological system. This God whom Job knows as the God over and beyond all the mystery of his own sufferings, who says 'yes' to his creature and from whom he does not want to be torn away, this is the God to whom he appeals as his witness, as vindicator and redeemer against the all wise theologizing of his friends, which could only appear to him as ridiculous.

The zeal which arises out of the affliction of his own life, draws its special sharpness from the seemingly pious speeches and claims on God of his friends, and is in its deepest intention a zeal for the living God. This then is the confirmation he finally hears from the mouth of the living one himself – that Job had spoken more correctly than his friends.

Besides this knowledge that Job had of the reality of God over against what humanly appears as clever doctrines about God, one would like to bring into the conversation with Bloch that revelation of the name of Yahweh, which he finds so important. If this *'ehyeh 'ašer 'ehyeh* is translated as 'I will be what I will be' and it is assumed that one can recognize the God who has futurity as a characteristic of his being, the *Deus Spes*, it might be well to set against this the grammatical insight of recent time which shrinks from speaking of the Hebrew perfect and imperfect as temporal in the sense of our idea of time, and prefers to identify the imperfect and perfect as aspects. But it would still hold true that here the Hebrew imperfect expresses the aspect of the continuing, the unforeclosed, in contrast to the established perfect. But more important is the fact that, in the etymology of the declaration of the name in Ex. 3.14, attention should be centred on the entire word sequence and not a single word, nor on the tense of the verbs used. The statement 'I am who I am' cannot be taken to express either a particular understanding of being or reality or a play upon the imperfect against the perfect. The whole figure is much more of a general statement turning back the question. It refuses in its literal sense to give an answer, much in the manner of Gen. 32.29. There the nocturnal figure with whom Jacob struggles answers Jacob's question about his name with the counter-question: 'Why do you ask about my name?' and so leaves Jacob's question unanswered. In the same way Ex. 3.14 should be understood as an imperious refusal by Yahweh. The particular thing which goes beyond the statement in Gen. 32.29 consists precisely in the *'ehyeh* which echoes the name of Yahweh, even in this sentence of refusal. For the understanding of the name of Yahweh this passage tells us that even there where he makes himself known by name and demonstrates his intention to save through the liberating act of the Exodus, he can never be built into a general relational system by human wisdom and theology or encapsulated by his name. But this is the God with whose incomprehensible freedom Job struggles and whom he defends as the true Lord against his friends who apparently know differently. The question is whether Bloch, when he talks about Job's exodus from God, because Job is the advocate of authentic humanity which he brings to his understanding of God, is not at the very bottom the advocate of a God of the manner of the pseudo-gods of the friends, who do not sense the living character of the truly living one.

The same question presses upon us when we move with Bloch beyond the realm of Old Testament discourse and speak of the New Testament, which he reads as a decline from the Old Testament, specifically with reference to his judgment of Jesus. When Bloch attempts to evaluate the New Testament proclamation of the kingdom of God by the 'Son of man' as the complete interjection of the human into the religious and as the complete exodus from God – does Bloch really sense here that the cry from the cross which he quotes, 'My God, My God, why hast thou forsaken me?', is made entirely in the direction of the cry of Job – not as a cry of exodus from God, but as a cry which just where everything comprehensible to man runs out, throws all into the hands of God – the God with the concealed face, who appears to be only wrath. Is Bloch conscious that God's surrender in the name of humanity, the surrender of that mysterious greater for that which is comprehensible to man, for the sake of a reasonable humanity, exists on the same level structurally with the pious friends of Job, who defend their foreknowledge with such wise arguments against the impenetrable reality of the one who in reality is God. The full biblical message of the friendliness of God to man can only be grasped at the point where the solidarity of God with man in the son of man is recognized in the depths of Job's experience.

Against this background, statements about a Creator also carry a completely different stress. The first thing to say here is that Bloch has really not hit on the emphasis of the creation account in Gen. 1. In that account there is no question of a justification of the world as it is today with all its injustice and evil, if the chapter is really to be read in the context of the historical sketch of the priestly writings as we presented it in chapter V. Bloch gives no attention to the fact that Gen. 1.31 must be read in the light of Gen. 6.11: 'Now the earth was corrupt in God's sight and the earth was filled with violence', even as for him, with all his passionate protest against the inhuman, the category of sin does not exist. Sin can be seriously comprehended only in a setting over against the Lord who commands responsibility, before whom that inhumanity only then receives its frightfully threatening character. But the *Deus Spes* is no real God before whom there is responsibility. He is man's own future of hope into which he rushes in ever newer rebellion against false standing-pat and harmful passivity and into which he knows himself drawn. In contrast to this it is an unalterable property of biblical speech, not only in Gen. 1, to know the one who is before absolutely all else, the one who has the power to call everything to account before him. It is out of the pathos of this knowledge that the prophetic proclamation arises with its revolutionary 'no' to the inhumanity stabilized and often religiously sanctioned in the world around. Because they know something of the Creator's affirmative to a world still intact, or, to put it in the categories of Job, the affirmative and desire of God towards his creature, who is intact in his intention, therefore they rebel right down the line against the damage to God's creature, and most of all the poor and lowly. Bloch's passion for the human undoubtedly touches a central nerve of biblical discourse. It misses this discourse, however, in that it does not recognize that this humanity experiences its deepest foundation in its creaturely stance before God, the Creator and the merciful one.

But here the place of the authentic foundation of human hope is also missed. A *Deus Spes* in which *Deus* is only a mask which must some day be thrown off means at last a loss of hope. Hope – and this Bloch has seen with all clarity – resides for man only in breaking out into what is new, in crossing the frontiers, in the leap into the other – only Bloch does not risk here the final radicality of formulation in which the step over the frontier, the way into newness, the leap into the other really means the transcending of all human possibilities. But this is what the Bible says as it speaks of the new creature, the new heaven and the new earth. Bloch's illumination of the Old Testament statements contains without a doubt an electrifying power. It forces a Bible reading that has become dull and that has comforted itself with a false spiritualization, or, to use Bloch's own formulation, 'the Christians with sleeping conscience', to hear and act anew. It strikes down that static outlook which believes that it can build God into a closed and finished picture of the world and which leads unquestioningly from such a static attitude to a retrospective one-sided conservative one. It remains however where it believes it sees the last goal as exodus from God, in that it appears to know only the God of yesterday who can be comprehended by thought and who is foreign to a full humanity, standing at the half-way point. It is closed to the fuller word of both Testaments according to which the Creator mercifully called his people out of slave-labour and in the Messiah made himself known in a yet more unfathomable solidarity with his creature fallen under death, and has called this creature into a future and a full hope. Where this biblical God is seen, then out of the transient God with futurity as his characteristic mode of being, out of the *Deus Spes*, there arises the *Deus Spei*. This God, whose characteristic mode of being is 'the first and the last', leads into a future and into the newness of the new creation, the new heaven and the new earth, into that genesis at the end. He leads into the future, which to use Bloch's beautiful concluding word, word for word in its first half, we will happily describe as 'that which everyone saw in childhood but no one ever really inhabited: home.'

NOTES

[1] See ch. I, n. I, p. 10 above.   [2] *Op. cit.*, p. I.
[3] *Ibid.*, p. 3.   [4] *Ibid.*, p. 6.   [5] *Ibid.*, p. 1628.
[6] *Ibid.*, pp. 575f.   [7] *Ibid.*, p. 576.   [8] *Ibid.*, p. 230.
[9] *Ibid.*, p. 1405.   [10] *Ibid.*, p. 1453.   [11] *Ibid.*, p. 1544.
[12] *Ibid.*, p. 1545.   [13] *Ibid.*, p. 1453.

[14] According to more recent views, Hammurabi is to be dated at the earliest in the eighteenth century BC.

[15] *Ibid.*, pp. 1453f.   [16] *Ibid.*, p. 1454.   [17] *Ibid.*, p. 1454.
[18] *Ibid.*, p. 1457.   [19] *Ibid.*, p. 1457.   [20] *Ibid.*, pp. 1457f.

[21] *Ibid.*, p. 576. On the Nazirites cf. Amos 2.11, also the story of Samson in Judges 13–16. In contrast to the family (not tribe) of the Rechabites, on whom cf. esp. Jer. 35, it is not possible historically to identify the Nazirites as a 'half-nomadic opposition'.

[22] *Ibid.*, p. 577.   [23] *Ibid.*, p. 577.   [24] *Ibid.*, p. 578.
[25] *Ibid.*, pp. 578f.   [26] *Ibid.*, p. 580.   [27] *Ibid.*, p. 1459.
[28] *Ibid.*, p. 713.   [29] *Ibid.*, pp. 888f.   [30] *Ibid.*, pp. 855f.
[31] *Ibid.*, p. 1392.   [32] *Ibid.*, p. 1410.   [33] *Ibid.*, p. 1410.
[34] *Ibid.*, p. 1410.   [35] *Ibid.*, p. 1410.   [36] *Ibid.*, p. 1411.
[37] *Ibid.*, p. 1412.   [38] *Ibid.*, p. 711.   [39] *Ibid.*, p. 1413.
[40] *Ibid.*, p. 1402.   [41] *Ibid.*, p. 1453.   [42] *Ibid.*, p. 1454.
[43] *Ibid.*, p. 1514.   [44] *Ibid.*, p. 1515.   [45] *Ibid.*, p. 1455.
[46] *Ibid.*, p. 1455.   [47] *Ibid.*, p. 1456.   [48] *Ibid.*, p. 1461.
[49] *Ibid.*, p. 1493.   [50] *Ibid.*, pp. 1496ff.

INDEXES

MODERN SCHOLARS

Alt, A., 84, 95, 105

Baumgartner, W., 11
Begrich, J., 41, 126, 137
Bloch, E., 1, 10, 61, ch. XI passim
Boer, P. de, 11
Briggs, C. A., 11
Brown, F., 11
Brunner, H., 25
Buhl, F., 6, 7, 9, 11
Bultmann, R., 2

Deissler, A., 29, 41
Driver, S. R., 11

Eichrodt, W., 10, 121
Elliger, K., 120, 137

Fohrer, G., 25, 105, 121, 137

Galling, K., 25, 121
Gemser, B., 25
Gese, H., 25
Gesenius, G., 6, 7, 9, 11
Gressmann, H., 105
Gunkel, H., 26, 27, 36, 41

Hempel, J., 25
Herrmann, S., 53, 55, 105, 111, 115, 117, 121
Hertzberg, H. W., 25
Horst, F., 120, 137

Kaiser, O., 105
Koehler, L., 4, 5, 6, 10, 11
Kraus, H. J., 41

Maag, V., 56, 68, 69
Marsch, W. D., 10
Mays, J. L., 105
McKane, W., 25
Moltmann, J., 10
Mowinckel, S., 26, 41

Noth, M., 55, 78, 79, 83, 84, 105

Ploeg, J. van der, 10
Ploeger, O., 150
Porteous, N., 150
Preuss, H. D., 11, 69
Pritchard, J. B., 41

Rad, G. von, 10, 57, 68, 69, 83, 84, 85, 88, 105, 137, 140, 150
Ringgren, H., 25
Robinson, T. H., 105, 150
Rohland, E., 105
Rowley, H. H., 150
Rudolph, W., 41, 121

Sauter, G., 10
Schmid, H. H., 75, 76, 77, 84
Smend, R., 69

Vriezen, T. C., 10

Weiser, A., 25, 41, 105, 121, 150
Westermann, C., 10, 26, 27, 36, 41, 137
Wildberger, H., 105
Wolff, H. W., 55, 83, 84, 85, 105, 150

Zimmerli, W., 25, 69, 121, 137

BIBLICAL REFERENCES

Genesis
ch. 1	21, 60, 61, 127, 157, 163
1.1	44
1.1–2.4a	60, 62
1.26	60
1.31	62, 157, 163
ch. 2	60
2.4b	44
2.7	119
2.17	45
2.18	45
2.23	45
ch. 3	47
3.4f.	46
3.16	47
3.19	46
3.20	47
ch. 4	47
4.14	48
4.15	48
6.1–4	48
6.5f.	48
6.11	62, 163
6.12	62
8.21f.	48
ch. 9	58, 62
ch. 12	49
12.1–3	49, 55
12.2f.	55
12.7	50
13.14ff.	50
ch. 15	51
ch. 17	58, 63, 65, 66
17.7	63
18.1ff.	51
ch. 23	63
23.4	64
ch. 24	51
25.7	51
25.9	64
26.3	51
26.24	51
28.3f.	65

Genesis
28.13f.	51
32.9	52
32.11f.	52
32.26	158
32.29	162
35.11f.	64
48.4	64
49.31	64
50.12f.	64

Exodus
3.7f.	52
3.14	155, 162
3.17	52
ch. 6	59
6.2f.	59
6.2–8	65
6.6b–7	65
12.11	124
13.21f.	124
14.4	67
14.20	124
ch. 16	66
16.6f.	67
16.12	67
17.1–7	124
20.22– 23.33	71
21.12	47
29.43–46	65
29.46	68
31.12f.	66

Leviticus
19.18	154

Numbers
11.11f.	53
11.14	53
14.4	53
20.1–13	124
21.9	160
chs. 22–24	54
24.15–17	54

Deuteronomy
chs. 1–3	79
chs. 1–11	71
chs. 1–30	71
6.1	72
6.5	77
7.8	73
8.1	73
8.7–10	73
9.5f.	74
11.13f.	73
ch. 12	74
chs. 12–26	71
12.1	72
12.8–10	74
16.3	124
25.4	2, 10
25.19	74
26.5–11	77
chs. 27–30	71
ch. 28	77
chs. 29–30	77
30.15f.	77

Joshua
ch. 1	78
1.13	79
7.26	93
ch. 12	79
ch. 23	78
23.1	79
23.6	80
23.14	79
23.15f.	79

Judges
2.11ff.	79, 80
2.12	80
chs. 13–16	165

Ruth
1.13	5

I Samuel
8.7	80

I Samuel
ch. 12   78, 80
12.20   80

II Samuel
ch. 7   81, 83
7.13a   81

I Kings
ch. 8   84
8.14ff.   78f.
8.15–53   81
8.46ff.   81
8.56   61
8.56–61   81
8.57f.   82
9.1ff.   82
9.9   82

II Kings
4.28   7
17.7ff.   79, 82
17.19f.   82
21.10–15   105
21.16   105
ch. 22   70

I Chronicles
29.15   112

Ezra
10.2   112

Nehemiah
2.13   5
2.15   5

Esther
9.1   5

Job
chs. 1–2   16
ch. 3   110
4.5–9   16
4.6   7
5.8–16   17
6.8f.   19
6.11f.   18
7.6   19
8.3–6   17
8.11–13   18

Job
11.14–20   18
13.13–16   22
14.1f.   19, 46f.
14.7ff.   19
14.13–15   22
14.19f.   19
16.2   32
16.18f.   23
17.11   6
ch. 19   91
19.10   19
19.25   23, 24
19.25–27   160
30.20, 26   20
chs. 32–37   16
ch. 42   16
42.7   20

Psalms
1   28
2   28
8   60
8.5–8   60
9.18   35
25   32
25.3   32
25.5   32
25.21   32
27   33, 35
27.14   35
31   35
33.3   125
33   36
33.18   36
33.20   36
33.22   36
37   29
37.1   14
37.8f.   29
37.34   29
38   32
38.15   32
39   37, 42
39.4   37
39.7f.   38
39.10f.   38
39.12b–13   37
40.1f.   35
40.4   125
42–43   33
46   99
48   99

Psalms
52   35
52.9   35
62.1   34
62.5   34
69   31
69.6   32
69.20   32
71   33
71.5   33
71.14   33
73   40, 91
73.17   40
73.23–26   40
76   99
96.1   125
104   36
104.27   5, 36
119   29, 31
119.43   30
119.49   6, 30
119.74   31
119.81   30
119.95   30
119.114   30
119.116   5, 30
119.147   30
119.166   5, 30
130   33
130.5f.   33
130.7   33
131   34
131.3   34
145.15   5, 36
146.5   5, 36
147.11   36

Proverbs
1.33   15
10.28   13
11.23   14
13.12   13
14.26   15
19.18   13
20.22   15
22.19   15
23.17f.   14
23.18   6, 14
24.13f.   14
24.14   7
24.19f.   14
26.12   15
29.20   15

Ecclesiastes

3.10f.	21
3.12f.	21
3.14	22
3.19f.	47
9.1ff.	20f.
9.4	7

Isaiah

1.4–9	96
1.5b–6	96
1.9	96
1.21–26	101
1.26	101
ch. 2	142
2.2–5	103
5.2b	97
5.4	97
5.7	97
ch. 6	95
6.11	96
ch. 7	90
8.16–18	98
8.20	6
8.23–9.6	105
9.4–5	102
9.6–7	102
10.5–7	98
10.12	98
10.23	146
11.1ff.	102
14.24ff.	98
14.27	104
14.28–32	100
17.12–14	105
chs. 24–27	143
24.4f.	143
24.23	143
25.6–8	144
28.16	100
28.21	100
28.22	146
29.1ff.	99
30.15	100
31.4f.	105
38.18	5
chs. 40–55	122
40.3–5	123f.
40.6–8	122
40.10f.	123
40.26	127
40.31	134
41.1ff.	127

Isaiah

41.4	128, 131
41.19	125
41.21–29	132
42.4	134
42.6	134
42.9	125, 133
42.10	125
ch. 43	124
43.8–13	131
43.9	131
43.10	132
43.16ff.	125
43.18ff.	133
44.5	129
44.6	131, 132
44.7f.	132
44.24–28	127
45.1–7	128
45.3	128
45.9	126
45.12f.	127
45.21	133
45.23f.	134
46.9–11	133
48.3f.	133
48.7	133
48.13	131
49.6	134
49.20	126
49.22f.	126
49.23	134
51.2	128
51.5	134
52.12	124
55.1–5	129
55.3–5	129
55.10f.	122
55.13	125
chs. 56–66	135
57.14f.	135
ch. 60	135
61.1f.	135
65.17	158

Jeremiah

1.8	116
1.10	111
1.19	116
3.6–13	78, 112
3.12f.	112f.
3.21–4.4	112
4.3f.	113

Jeremiah

4.14	113
4.19–21	109f.
6.8	113
12.11	115
14.1–15.4	112
14.8	112
14.19b	112
14.22	112
15.15–21	115
15.20	116
17.5–8	28
17.13	112
20.9	110
20.14–18	110f.
23.5f.	115, 136
25.11f.	145
26.18	94
29.10	145
29.10–14	114
29.11	6
chs. 30f.	112, 115
ch. 31	119
31.15–17	113
31.31–34	115
ch. 32	114
32.15	114
33.15f.	114
ch. 35	165
35.19	116
ch. 36	113
36.3	113, 114
36.7	113
39.17f.	116
45.5	116
50.7	112

Lamentations

ch. 3	38
3.18	38
3.18–29	38
3.21	38
3.22–24	84
3.29	84

Ezekiel

1.1	70
ch. 7	116
chs. 8–11	120
11.14–21	119
ch. 16	117
17.22–24	119
19.5	120

Ezekiel
ch. 20   117, 123
20.32ff.   119, 123
27.1ff.   118
33.10   117
ch. 34   119
ch. 36   119
36.16ff.   117
36.22f.   118
37.7f.   118
37.10   118
37.11   117, 120
37.12   119
37.14   119
37.27f.   119
chs. 38f.   141
chs. 39f.   141
chs. 40–48   120
40.3ff.   140
43.7   120
ch. 47   144
47.1–12   120

Daniel
chs. 1–6   149
ch. 2   59, 144, 145,
              147
2.4b–7.28   144
2.44   148
3.17f.   150
ch. 5   144
ch. 7   59, 145, 147,
              148
7.14   148
7.27   148
ch. 8   145, 146
8.14   146
8.25   146
ch. 9   139, 145
              146, 148
9.27   146
chs. 10–12   145
10.21   149
ch. 11   146
11.45   146
12.1   148, 149
12.2f.   148
12.11   146
12.12   146

Hosea
1.2   92

Hosea
1.6   92
1.9   92
2.14f.   93
2.20f.   93
3.3–5   92
5.8–8.6   105
5.13   91
5.14   90
6.1–3   91
6.4   91
6.6   92
ch. 11   93
11.8f.   92
12.9   93

Joel
ch. 1   142
1.2   143
ch. 2   142
2.2   143
3.15f.   142

Amos
2.5–7   156
2.11   165
3.1f.   88f.
5.14f.   89
5.18–20   88
7.1–3   142
8.2   89
9.7   89
9.11f.   90
9.13–15   90

Jonah
4   130

Micah
1.5   94
2.1–5   95, 105
2.5   95
3.12   94
4.1–4   103
5.2–6   94f.
7.7   6

Nahum
1.15   106
2.2   106

Habakkuk
2.4   106

Habakkuk
3.13   106
3.18   106

Zephaniah
chs. 1–2   108
2.3   108
3.12f.   108

Zechariah
1.7ff.   140
3.1–7   137
6.9–15   137

Malachi
3.23   136
4.5   140

Matthew
2.6   94

John
3.14   160

Acts
13.33   28

Romans
5.3–5   3
ch. 8   3

I Corinthians
9.10   2
13.13   3

Philippians
1.6   34

I Thessalonians
4.13   3

Hebrews
ch. 11   3

I Peter
3.15   3

Revelation
13.10   149
20.8f.   142
21.2   157